MARYLAND
SEPTEMBER

TRUE STORIES FROM THE
ANTIETAM CAMPAIGN

Thomas McGrath

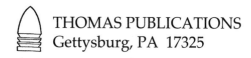

THOMAS PUBLICATIONS
Gettysburg, PA 17325

To my family,
and
Lindy

ACKNOWLEDGEMENTS

My thanks go to Linda Donaldson for all of her help and encouragement. Also to the Microtext Staff at the Boston Public Library, John Ray of Sharpsburg, Maryland, and of course to all of the people at Thomas Publications who made this book possible.

CONTENTS

Introduction
1

Part I
The Campaign:
September 5 – 13, 1862
3

Part II
South Mountain to Sharpsburg, Maryland:
September 14 – 15, 1862
14

Part III
Cannonade and Battle:
September 16 – 17, 1862
28

Part IV
Aftermath
58

The Sources
76

Photo Credits

INTRODUCTION

When studying the events of the Civil War, it is easy to become preoccupied and even a bit overwhelmed by the strategic aspect of the armies and their commanders. Although analysis of maps, troop movements, strengths, and positions is essential to understanding these events from a tactical point of view, to see the whole picture they must also be examined on a much smaller scale.

Each army, though acting as one mass, was made up of individual men of vastly different backgrounds, character, and personality. To use simple expressions like "McClellan marched from Frederick to South Mountain" or, "Jackson surrounded Harpers Ferry" can be misleading. Movements such as these involved tens of thousands of men. Every one of these men had a story to tell, each one different from the rest.

The true "reality" of war can only be found in the words of the men and women who lived it. It is important to examine what happened from an "eye-level" point of view. Travel the dusty roads with them and see what they saw. Listen to the banter, the joking, and the laughing, as well as the crying and moaning. Discover how the many new recruits, just average young men fresh from their small hometowns and farms, tried to cope with what it meant to be a soldier at war. All of this was a part of those tremendous weeks of late summer and early autumn of 1862, the period of the Antietam Campaign.

The stories in *Maryland September* approach the events of this extraordinary campaign from that "eye-level" point of view. Some of them were found in newspapers, or second-hand accounts, but most are from the writings of the men themselves, either from battle diaries or personal memoirs. The reader will travel with these soldiers, both Union and Confederate, on the hot, dry march through Maryland, through the occupation of Frederick, the savage battles of South Mountain and Antietam, and the indescribable horrors of the gruesome aftermath. A glimpse is given of the ordinary citizens who, as fate would have it, found themselves and their families directly in the path of two massive armies as they cut a swathe of destruction through their otherwise peaceful world.

In so many reminiscences the emotion comes through and hits home with striking clarity, helping to shatter the image portrayed of these people, stiffly posed in old black and white photographs. The words

1

inject color, thought, and movement into a portrait of this era. These people were much like ourselves in that they felt fear, joy, excitement, and sorrow. Also, as evident by the fact that so many took the time to write out their experiences in such detail, the tremendous effect which these events had on their lives, echoes of which are still being felt today, can be felt. We will never know all of their stories, but the more we do, the clearer the picture becomes as to what actually happened to these people, soldiers and civilians, when the war came to the rolling hills and peaceful farmlands of Maryland, in September of 1862.

In an engagement where there were so many casualties, no man knew when his turn might come, and many incidents are told in the diaries and letters of the men, of narrow escapes and queer happenings of the field; things that to outsiders might seem trivial, but to men whose lives were hanging by a thread, everything was of importance.

—E.O. Lord, 1895
History of the 9th New Hampshire Volunteers

On the morning of September 5, 1862 the first elements of General Robert E. Lee's Army of Northern Virginia slipped across the Potomac River to begin their invasion of Maryland. The Federal Army at this time was camped in and around Washington, having just suffered defeat at the Battle of Second Bull Run. Within days, under the leadership of their beloved General George McClellan, the Union Army marched northward in pursuit of the invading Rebel Army. The Antietam Campaign had begun.

PART I

THE CAMPAIGN:
SEPTEMBER 5-13, 1862

A Rude Awakening

On their march to Frederick, Maryland, members of the Union "Irish Brigade" spent the night on a field covered with fresh haystacks. In the morning a soldier who had slept on top of one of these haystacks slid down and landed hard on a soldier sleeping below. "You scoundrel!" shouted the man in the hay.

"You've broken my ribs. Who the devil are you?" The standing soldier responded by giving the protesting man a swift kick and shouting, "And who the devil are you? Get up out of that." When the man rose the soldier stepped back. The fellow he had just kicked was none other than Major General Israel B. Richardson, Division Commander. "Well bless my soul," exclaimed the soldier in awe, "it's General Richardson! Who'd have thought I was kicking you? I am sorry, sir, I assure you." Then, trying to redeem himself, he pulled a flask from his coat and said, "Here, sir, have a drink with me. It's good stuff and the morning air's a little sharp." General Richardson now recognized the man as captain Jack Gosson. "Captain Jack!" he replied. "Well, of course, you couldn't tell who it was under the hay. I think I will join you in something to keep the chill off, while we're going over to breakfast."

Major General Israel B. Richardson

GRABBING THE BULL BY THE HORNS

While marching through Maryland, members of the Ninth New Hampshire came upon a drove of government cattle. As they passed, the drover was having a difficult time with one particularly unruly bull. After several taunts by the New Hampshire men, the drover said that if they could catch him, they could have him. No sooner said than done, two daring men from the regiment named Reuben and Wentworth immediately stepped out of line and literally "took the bull by the horns," and "in less than thirty minutes his inanimate carcass, as neatly dressed as if for some fashionable butcher's shop, was ready for dissection and distribution as an extra ration of fresh beef." Private Reuben was subsequently "promoted to the nominal rank of brigade butcher—an office with certain gastronomical perquisites, if no increase in pay."

COW AND CALF

Two Confederate soldiers, while entering Frederick, Maryland, came across a man named Joe Shaner, "the most noted forager in the battery, on his way to camp with a bag of eatables across his shoulder and a canteen of old apple jack slung around his neck." One of the rebels, by the name of Ned, insisted on taking a swig of the apple jack, but Joe refused to take off his cumbersome load to oblige him. So the two made a compromise. Joe, who was short, stood there while thirsty Ned, who was over six feet tall, dropped to his knees to drink from the canteen. Men passing by took one look at this ridiculous spectacle and called out, "Just look at that old cow and calf!" And everyone within earshot had a good laugh.

SLEEPY STONEWALL

This newspaper article, which refers to the renowned and revered Confederate General Thomas J. "Stonewall" Jackson, is from the Frederick *Examiner*, 1862:

> Sunday, 7 inst. (September)... Gen. Jackson attended worship in the evening, at the Evan. Ref. Church and fell asleep during the service.

Major General "Stonewall" Jackson

5

A Scrap Over Water

It was early September 1862, and two great armies were marching over the dirt roads of Maryland. It had not rained for some time and on this hot, dry, dusty march water became a rare and precious commodity. When the occasional well or stream was encountered, and the order came to "fall out," these places would often be the scene of much pushing, shoving, and brawling between men trying to fill their canteens. A Pennsylvania colonel related: "On our second or third day's march, such a scrap took place between the advanced columns for a well, and in the melee one man was accidentally pushed down into it, head first, and killed. He belonged to one of those Connecticut regiments, I was told. We passed by the well, and were unable to get water, because a dead soldier lay at the bottom of it. His regiment probably got his body out, but we had to march on without stopping to learn whether they did or not."

A Macabre Gift

A resident of Frederick, Maryland relates a rather bizarre incident which occurred as Confederate troops marched through his town.

Several young ladies were standing in front of the house of one of our prominent citizens, when a rebel officer rode up and, halting his horse, said, "Ladies, allow me to make you a present." And with that he extended his hand, a small object clenched between two fingers, "This is a ring made from the bone of a dead Yankee." A gentleman, near the curb, seized the article before the officer had finished speaking...The ladies...quickly answered, "Keep your present for those who appreciate such presents." The only reply of the chivalry was, "Ah! I supposed you were Southern ladies!" This incident is instructive.

A Maryland Maiden Reconsiders

J.E.D. Ward, a member of the 12th Ohio Volunteer Infantry, tells this humorous story, which happened on the march into Maryland.

...the task of driving the rebels was extremely laborious, yet the gallant troops who accomplished the duty, felt themselves to be more than recompensed in the grateful demeanor of the citizens, particularly among the females, who were delighted even to wildness. They caught up and kissed hundreds of dusty, travel-begrimed soldiers, hugging them as if they were endeared by ties more binding than simple gratitude...One young lady in the intoxication of joy, jumped up and declared that she could kiss the whole army. A *grizzly* old sergeant who overheard her remark, at once proposed that she start on him. On second thought, however, she declined the proceeding.

RAILS

The following story comes from Corporal Nelson Hutchinson of the 7th Massachusetts Infantry:

One night about an hour before sunset we were halted in a field enclosed with a high snake-fence on the outskirts of Jefferson [Md]. Col. Russel told us that we would stop here a short time, and march all night. "So make your little fires, and cook your little coffee, men, but don't touch the rail fence." The fence was all the available wood in sight, so some of the men [complained] to the commander. "Well," said he, "you can take the top rail [only]." When I got around to the fence, the top rails, and more, were gone; and while I was weighing the probabilities of getting snubbed if I filched another rail, a man stepped up, and took one off. "Here! Here!" said the colonel, "didn't I tell you to take only the top rail?" With the utmost nonchalance the man put the rail back, then stepped away, and struck an attitude with both arms spread out, and exclaimed, "There, colonel! Isn't that the top rail?" The official was outflanked, and replied with a wavering voice, 'Oh, take it away, dem ya! you would take the bottom rail and then swear it was the top one." Then I took a ration of rail; and, when we got through with that fence, the bottom rails were the top ones.

7

A Bit Too Cocky

Ahead of the Confederate infantry, a "group of fifteen horsemen" rode into Middletown, Md. on September 8 around noon. Their leader was "Capt." Edward Motter, himself a native of that county. Immediately they began to create a ruckus. After tearing down and mutilating a Union flag, the rebels boasted to everyone that they were in search of Capt. Cole's Union Cavalry, quite a challenge for a mere fifteen horsemen. After a few hours the rowdy bunch retired to a local tavern and proceeded to enjoy the generous hospitality of the tavern's owner. Apparently they had too good a time, for as they were swilling beers and recalling their "courageous" foray, a group of Union Cavalry, under a Captain Russel, surprised the party and captured fourteen of them. "The people [of Middletown], especially the females, were wild with enthusiasm." The rebels probably would have escaped except that "a number of them" were "so drunk that they overstaid their time." Oddly, the only one who got away was Capt. Motter himself.

Dirty Army

"I have never seen a mass of such filthy, strong smelling men," a resident of Frederick, Maryland said, describing the appearance of the Rebel army as it marched through his town. "Three of them in a room would make it unbearable..." This same resident encountered six young men from a neighboring county who, like hundreds of others, had converged on Frederick with dreams of becoming a soldier under Robert E. Lee. After "seeing and smelling" the famed Army of Northern Virginia, however, they decided to return home.

Another witness also spoke of the obvious prevalence of body lice, judging, he said, "from the animated nature of their persons." Other accounts depict soldiers in the street picking the lice off each other. This ailment was a problem for both armies.

Strange Boast

While in Frederick, a Confederate officer boasted to a lady that he would "kill, cut up, and fry a Yankee with as much pleasure as he would a chicken." Hearing this in wide-eyed disbelief, a young slave girl exclaimed, "And, massa, would you eat him, too?"

MAD LANTZ

The following story, from the journal of William Harrer, a New York private, refers to one of his fellow soldiers who had somewhat of a "psychotic" nature. It occurred on the march through Maryland, a few miles south of Frederick.

It was now about four o'clock in the afternoon when we passed by the road-side a small farm-house. A lady was standing in front and we asked her to sell us some potatoes, which we saw growing in her little garden.

"Dig all you want for a meal," she said. We paid the good woman for them, went back in her apple orchard, started a good fire, put on our potatoes in one cup and our coffee in the other. But Lantz was not satisfied yet. He wanted milk for our coffee, and off he started with his canteen to a nice-looking house on the other side of the road.

"There," he said, "I can get what we want." While he was away I attended to the cooking operations, but after about fifteen minutes he came back raving. He took his gun, fixed bayonet and started running toward the farm-house. Not understanding what he meant to do, I ran after him and took him by the arm, saying:

"What are you going to do?"

"Shoot that farmer. He told me to get off his farm as quick as I could. And no milk. I'll go over and shoot him."

He would have done it, for this man Lantz sometimes got out of his latitude. He would go fairly mad and froth at the mouth with uncontrolled rage. I quieted him down, telling him how well off we were since we had potatoes, coffee, hard-tack, and pork. We ate our dinner and went on again for a few miles.

FINE BUSINESS

Mr. A. J. Delashman was a leading Secessionist in Frederick and one of the few citizens who rejoiced at the arrival of the Rebel army in this predominantly Union county. He and a few others went out and personally welcomed the troops as they marched into town. Delashman soon had a change of heart, however, when the army bought out his large stock of shoes and boots in exchange for worthless Confederate money. It was said he "fairly grit his teeth in silence when some of his Union friends congratulated him on the fine business he was doing."

A rooftop view of Frederick, Maryland taken just after the war.

"DAMNABLY DECEIVED"

Upon trying to purchase goods at a Frederick store, a Rebel colonel was told by the store's owner that his Confederate notes were "not worth the paper they were printed on." Hearing this the colonel asked the merchant what his political views were.

"I am a Union man, Sir, and always intend to remain one," replied the storekeeper firmly.

"Indeed!" remarked the Colonel. "Are there many people like you here?"

"Yes, Sir. We have voted on secession, and this district gave three thousand majority for the Union."

"Yes, at the point of the bayonet!" the colonel insinuated.

"No, Sir," insisted the shopkeeper, "there were neither bayonets nor muskets to intimidate us. Every man was free to vote as he pleased."

The Colonel claimed that they had received thousands of letters from Maryland begging to be saved from the oppressive "Lincoln Government." But since their arrival they had been treated "damned cooly" by the people here. Realizing the true state of affairs the exasperated Colonel could only say, "Then we have been most damnably deceived. I feel like hell."

JACKSON AND BRANDY

The eccentric but brilliant commander Thomas J. "Stonewall" Jackson was known never to touch liquor. That is what makes the following incident, which occurred in Frederick, so intriguing. "Early in the day, outside of town, one of the citizens gave Jackson a large gray mare. Little Sorrel [Jackson's horse] had been stolen. The first time he mounted the mare she threw him. An officer poured him out a drink of brandy, and Old Jack, shaken by his fall, drank it off. "I've always liked it," he said. "That's why I let it alone. I fear it more than Yankee bullets."

HORSE FOR SALE

During the Confederate occupation of Frederick, one clever young boy took advantage of the situation and made a quick profit. He had recently purchased a condemned horse from the Federal government which he had hoped to nurse back to good health. For the first two days, however, the horse refused to eat, and his condition worsened.

When the Rebels entered town, one of the soldiers approached the boy and asked if he had a horse for sale. "Well, yes," replied the boy firmly, "worth two hundred dollars to any man who can prize a good horse." The rebel asked to see the horse. To this the boy answered, "No sir! He is a spirited animal and might do a stranger some injury. Let me bring him out for you." The youth then proceeded to fetch the animal from the stable. When he showed the beast to the prospective buyer the boy added, "I've given it some thought, and have decided to let you have this magnificent animal for eighty dollars in U.S. money, not Confederate script."

The rebel looked at the beast and remarked, "But look at him. He only stands on three legs. Why is that?"

The clever boy replied, "Why, Lord bless you! Don't you understand that? He is a *natural racker*; all natural rackers stand on three legs that way—always."

The rebel, thinking he was getting a steal, paid the boy his money, and rode off on his new horse, "somewhat to the seller's astonishment." The boy remarked to a group of onlookers, "I pledge you my word, gentlemen, he will last about three quarters of an hour at least. Any other gentleman wanting a natural racker can be accommodated at the shortest notice, if he will only call on me."

DINNER AT A "REB" HOUSE

Although Frederick was a town of strong Union sympathies, a colonel of the 132nd Pennsylvania named Frederick Hitchcock remembers enjoying the hospitality of a Secessionist family during his stay there. The farmer was not shy in voicing his opinions to his guest:

> This night I succeeded in getting a "bang up" supper—a cooked meal—at a reb farm-house. It consisted of porksteak, potatoes, and hot coffee with bread and butter. It was a great treat. I had now been without a square meal for nearly ten days. The old gentleman, a small farmer, talked freely about the war, not concealing his rebel sympathies. He extolled Stonewall Jackson and his men, who, he said, had passed through there only a day ahead of us. He firmly believed we would be whipped. He evidently had an eye for the "main chance," for he was quite willing to cook for us at twenty-five cents at meal, as long as he had stuff to cook and his good wife had strength to do the work. She seemed to be a nice old lady, and, hungry as I was, I felt almost unwilling to eat her supper, she looked so tired. I told her it was too bad. She smiled and said she was tired, but she couldn't bear to turn away these hungry boys. She said she had a son in the rebel army, and she knew we must be hungry and wet, for it was still raining hard.

THE GENERAL'S KISS

While in Frederick, the Union troops were treated as heroes by the townspeople. Doors and windows opened, banners flew, and the citizens cheered as the boys in blue marched through the town. At one point, a "handsome, middle-aged lady" stepped out of her house and approached General Burnside, who sat astride his horse. She grabbed the general's hand and stood on her toes to give him a kiss.

> The general so understood her, and, doffing his hat, bent down to meet her pouting lips, but, alas, he was too high up; bend as low as he might and stretch up as high as she could,

their lips did not meet, and the kiss hung in mid-air. The boys caught the situation in a moment, and began to laugh and clap their hands, but the general solved the problem by dismounting and taking his kiss in the most gallant fashion, on which he was roundly cheered by the men. The lady was evidently of one of the best families. She said she was a staunch Union woman, and was so glad too see our troops that she felt she must greet our general. There was 'method in her madness,' however, for she confined her favors to a general, and picked out the handsomest one of the lot. It is worthy of note, that during this incident, which excited uproarious laughter, not a disrespectful remark was made by any of the hundreds of our 'boys' who witnessed it. General Burnside chatted with her for a few moments, then remounted and rode away.

Major General Ambrose Burnside

CONFEDERATE PUNISHMENT

According to the recollections of James Stone of the 21st Massachusetts, General Stonewall Jackson was as severe in punishment as he was brazen in battle. As the 21st was marching to Middletown, Maryland on the afternoon of September 13, they passed "two Johnnies hanging from the branch of a tree in a pasture a few rods from the road. They had been executed for foraging by Stonewall Jackson's orders." This story is corroborated by at least one other Union soldier in his own diary.

WHERE'S JOHN CONLEY?

It was midnight of the 13th when the 17th Michigan reached Middletown, Maryland after a rapid march. The men were exhausted and "hungry as wolves." They had just stacked arms for the evening when Lieutenant Rath of the regiment approached them. "Where's John Conley?" he asked. The men said they didn't know. "Well, then," said Rath, "send me the next best thief; I want a chicken for my supper."

By September 14, General Lee's Confederate Army of Northern Virginia was split into three separate bodies which were spread out over a wide area west of South Mountain. General McClellan, learning of Lee's vulnerability, decided to attack. A tiny fraction of the Confederate Army was in the vicinity of South Mountain as the Union Army approached. It would be up to this small force to hold off the entire Federal Army while the Confederates could regroup. The fighting that occurred on the steep wooded hillsides would later be called the Battle of South Mountain, and incredibly for the Confederates, it worked.

PART II

SOUTH MOUNTAIN TO SHARPSBURG, MARYLAND: SEPTEMBER 14-15, 1862

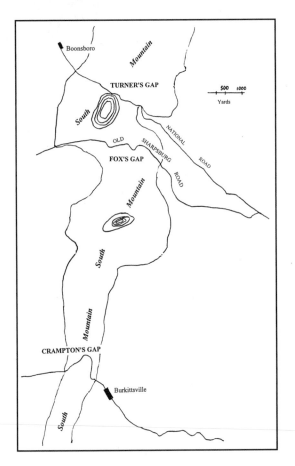

THE TREE

During the skirmishing preceding the battle for South Mountain, soldiers of both armies were witness to a bizarre encounter. A Confederate soldier in the advance of his company, ran to the shelter of a large chestnut tree. At the same time, a Yankee soldier ran to the same tree from the opposite side. The two enemies then jumped from behind the tree, leveled their rifles at each other, and fired at point blank range. The rebel fell dead in his tracks and the Yankee had his hat blown off his head but miraculously escaped unharmed.

JARRED JOKESTER

The following incident happened to a Pennsylvania volunteer during the battle for South Mountain and is told here in his own words:

Quite a scene was witnessed by one of our troop's [in] action. Thear was a solid Ball fired at us from the enemy & it struck short & roaled along the field & [it] appeared to be almost stopped when one of our Soldiers ran afrunt of it and put his foot square on it & it tossed him head over heals. He done it in a Joke but it was serious to him as he was so severely Jarred that he had to be taken to the Hospital.

DEADLY DILEMMA

While waiting for orders to charge the Confederate defenses on September 14, members of the 12th Ohio laid crouched behind a stone wall, hiding from rebel bullets. Suddenly, a rattlesnake made its appearance and began slithering over the men, "getting inside their clothes, and performing in various other disagreeable ways, to their infinite horror and disgust." It was a very unnerving predicament. If any one showed any part of his body, he risked being shot. If he did nothing, however, he might die a slow, agonizing death due to a poisonous snake bite. As the snake brushed his scaly skin over one soldier, the man could not bear it any longer. Quickly, he jumped up and rammed the butt of his rifle into the snake's head several times, killing it. Luckily for him, he did not draw the rebels' attention and returned to his place in line unharmed, and rid of the snake.

ONE ON ONE

During the battle of South Mountain, a Vermont soldier fell while climbing over a ledge. After tumbling down the slope eighteen or twenty feet, he stood up to find himself face to face with a Confederate, in a somewhat isolated position on the battlefield. At first, they just glared at each other. Then the "Reb," realizing the awkwardness of the situation, burst out laughing. "We're both in a fix!" he exclaimed. "You can't gobble me, and I can't gobble you, till we know which is going to lick. Let's wait till the shooting is over, and if your side wins, I'm your prisoner; and if we win, you're my prisoner!" So the agreement was made. "But," said the Vermonter after the Union army took the mountain, "didn't that reb feel cheap when he found I'd won him!"

BRAVE REBEL COLOR SERGEANT

The "Battle Flag" played an important role in the Civil War. Each regiment had its own colors on which they dedicated their loyalty, faith, and fierce allegiance. It represented who they were, where they came from, and, in essence, the battle flags themselves were what these men fought for. There are countless tales of bravery in battle associated with the flags and many good men were killed in trying to save their regiment's pride and honor. The following incident, which occurred near Fox's Gap on South Mountain, was remembered by a member of the 12th Ohio. It speaks much of the men of both sides:

> A rebel color sergeant, being surrounded, tore off the flag he was carrying and wrapped it around his body. Commanded to surrender, he replied, "Gentlemen, I am a color sergeant and can not surrender." At the same time he jerked out a revolver and began firing. In an instant a dozen balls pierced his body and he fell dead. It was an instance of rash heroism which was admired by all who witnessed it, and those who shot him did it with tears in their eyes."

The 23rd and 12th Ohio fighting at Fox's Gap

16

A Young Yankee Loses His Nerve

Not every soldier was able to face up to his duty when he came under fire. Before charging the steep slopes at Crampton's Gap, members of the 5th Maine were ordered to lie down for better protection. George Bicknell remembered what turned out to be an amusing incident that occurred during this time:

> It was in the midst of a grand chorus of bullets that one recruit, whose courage had entirely leaked out of his boots, dropped his musket, and had just started upon a full trot to the rear, when he was halted by an officer who inquired his reason for going to the rear. The demoralized youth, with frightened visage and disheveled locks, tremblingly cried out, "du ye 'spose I'm guine to stay here and get w-a-u-n-d-e-d?" and immediately broke into a full gallop for a less dangerous neighborhood. The ludicrous nature of this case restrained any enforcement of discipline, causing even the missiles of death to be forgotten for a moment, while shouts of laughter came from all who witnessed the fun.

Eerie Premonitions

A private of the 6th Wisconsin recalled a strange occurrence on September 14, as his regiment was marching towards South Mountain:

> It took us until the next Sunday to get to Middleto[w]n, Md., where we stopped at noon to make coffee. Geo. Miles, who was as brave a man as ever lived and wore the blue, was for him very serious, not his usual jolly self at all. We all noticed it. We asked him why he was so quiet, so unusual for him who was generally the life of the company. He replied: "You fellows would be quiet too, if you knew you would be killed tonight." We all laughed at him and told him we had been chasing Rebels for a week now, and had seen none and that there was about as much of a chance of a fight as there was of going home then.

That evening, the 6th Wisconsin was engaged in the fighting north of Turner's Gap on South Mountain. At a point about halfway up the mountain, brave George Miles was struck by a bullet and killed. The recorder of this prophetic event, added in his writings, "This incident is related here because four other just such predictions were made by members of the company at various times and all came when there was apparently nothing to suggest the possibility when the prediction was made. These premonitions, as they are called, often occurred, but who can explain the phenomena that produces the same—not the writers of this."

STRANGE COINCIDENCE

There was a story related to a local newspaper by a "very respectable citizen" of Middletown, Maryland concerning Major General Jesse Reno of the Union Army. Reno commanded the Federal Ninth Corps as it tried to push itself over South Mountain on September 14 in the face of a fierce Rebel resistance. The story goes that as the General was approaching the battle he was riding in an ambulance. At one point he turned to a friend next to him and said half-jokingly how odd it would be if that same ambulance were to remove his remains from the field. Early the next morning, that very same ambulance rolled solemnly into the streets of Middletown, Maryland bearing the dead body of Major General Jesse Reno, killed in action at Fox's Gap.

Major General Jesse Reno

KNAPSACKS

Following the Battle of South Mountain, members of Company B, 48th Pennsylvania "captured" a large number of knapsacks that had belonged to the Rebels. Due to the Confederates' recent victory at Second Bull Run and the march through unscathed Maryland, the knapsacks were full of practical spoils of war. This included many clean or new shirts, stockings and drawers. The Pennsylvania captain had his men change into these items then and there. He did this, however, in small groups so that his men would not be surprised by the enemy and driven from the field buck naked.

By an amazing coincidence, a number of the knapsacks were inscribed with the regiment's own insignia, having been "captured" from them at the last battle. The men felt great satisfaction in regaining their old packs and joked, "Now we are even with the Johnnys in [the] capturing of Knapsacks."

A member of the 13th Massachusetts also remembered a similar incident of that same battle. "One of our boys, regretting the loss of his knapsack, and noticing the Reb had one, concluded to make good his loss by transferring it to his own back. Now the most astonishing thing about this was the discovery, upon removing the knapsack, that it was his own property, which had been toted from Manassas to South Mountain by a rebel soldier. He was still more amazed on opening it to find the contents had been undisturbed."

Confused "Billy" Fitzpatrick

A servant to a Union captain, known to the men as "Billy," was walking across the slopes of South Mountain, observing the dead bodies of both sides when he came across a particularly odd looking group of dead rebels lying behind a stone wall. Perplexed, he soon returned to the captain. "Well, Billy, did you see them?" asked the Captain.

"O, trouth I did," replied Billy, "but, Captain, isn't them strange men?"

"Why?" asked the Captain.

"Be my soul, every man of them has a third eye in his head."

The Captain then laughed and explained that those men had all been shot in the head.

A Confederate Surrenders

Searching over the battlefield in an area north of Turner's Gap, a private of the 76th New York found a "long, gaunt 'gray-back,' about seventeen years of age" hiding unarmed behind a stump. When the Southerner saw the soldier standing over him he stood up and exclaimed, "Don't shoot! Don't shoot! I'm your prisoner."

The frightened boy was taken in and explained to his captors that he had never wanted to join the Rebel army, but was forced to. "I told 'em I was a coward and couldn't fight, but they drove me up here, where I came near being killed; so I dropped, and crawled and waited there all night."

Brave Decision

The day after the Battle of South Mountain, the First Corps of the Army of the Potomac began marching towards the small town of Boonsboro on the National Turnpike. Near the head of the column was Ben Van Valkenburg, a corporal from the 76th New York, now on General Abner Doubleday's staff. Riding on horseback, he spotted a farm house about a mile off in the distance, and with "visions of chickens and other contraband" he spurred his horse on and galloped ahead of the column. Soon, he alone was ahead of the entire army. Reaching the farm, he rode into the yard and around to the back of the house.

Suddenly, he stopped dead in his tracks. Sitting on the porch glaring at him, were seven "stalwart rebels," with their rifles by their sides!

An awkward moment of silence hung heavily in the air as no one dared to move a muscle. Ben later admitted he was "mightily scared" at this point. What would happen next? If he turned and ran he knew that would only mean seven bullets in his back and that was "a portion of Ben's body which could not with his consent be thus desecrated." So with all of his might, he whipped out his revolver and shouted, "All of you, now, surrender!!" Six rifles fell to the ground. One Rebel, however, held out. Ben rode up to the stubborn soldier and leveled his gun at his head, saying, "You have thirty seconds to decide your fate." The Confederate, uttering a "bitter oath," reluctantly dropped his gun.

After some prodding, the prisoners were formed into line. While marching out through the gate of the yard, two more "well-armed" Rebels suddenly appeared. Ben ordered them to "Fall in!" and they, thinking the men were Union skirmishers, dropped their guns and joined their fellow southerners.

General Doubleday was so impressed with Ben's act of bravery that he offered him an officer's commission. The humble New Yorker respectfully declined, however, replying, "I am much obliged to you General, but I am uneducated and unfitted for an office. I came here to fight, and that I am willing to do." From then on, Ben was a favorite at Division headquarters.

REBEL BOOTS

Near the Wise Farm on South Mountain a dead Confederate soldier was sitting astride a stone wall. A passing Federal soldier spotted the man and despite the gruesome spectacle managed to joke, "That's the first rebel I've seen with a decent pair of boots on, and by thunder, if he ha'n't got up there to show 'em off!"

Dead Confederates across from the Wise Farm house, Fox's Gap.

HOSPITAL SCENE

A Union soldier, in his own words, gives us this account of what he saw after the fighting for South Mountain was done, and the true agony of war for many had begun. For many new recruits who had recently enlisted, this Maryland mountain top was where they first saw the almost surreal horrors of war. And it was a place none of them would ever forget:

> At this place, being the top of South Mountain, the Hospital was an awful sight, being a little house, by itself, & in the yard thear was 3 or 4 large tables in it & as the soldiers was put on it (that was wounded), the surgical Corps Came along & the head of the Corps had in his hand a piece of White Chalk & he marked the place whear the Limb was to be Cut off & right behind him was the line of surgeons with thear instruments & [they] proceeded to amputate &... Looking around in the yard, I saw a Beautiful, plump arm Laying [there], which Drew my attention & in looking a Little [at] it, and seeing another of the same kind, I picked them up & Laid them together & found that they are a right [arm] & one a Left Arm, which Convinced me that they war off the one man & you could see many legs Laying in the yard with the shoes & stockings on—not taken off when amputated...

THE OLD COCK

A federal soldier passing through Frederick gives us this account of a rather unusual chance meeting. It is a good example of the taunting that went on between the armies:

> As we passed through Frederick on the morning of the fifteenth, we halted for a short time in one of the main streets...On the sidewalks were many prisoners who had just been sent in from the field of South Mountain. Among them were some North Carolinians, as slim as a lath and as tall as a church spire. They were gathered in groups. Pretty soon, two of their number, who seemed to be pointing out and gesticulating toward our Colonel, drawled out in the usual "Tar-heel" vernacular, "I say, Bill, thar's the 'old cock' we uns had a prisoner at Richmond." The other looked again, and nodding assent, replied loudly, "I reckon you uns is right." The Colonel pricked up his ears...He turned his angry face toward the elongated "Tar-heelers," and with a strong, nasal twang, for which he was noted, said, "Yes, you d—d scoundrels! I'm the same 'old cock' but blank! blank! you'll never get him there again!"

LATE NIGHT FEAST

David L. Thompson, Company G, of the Ninth New York, tells of the night spent in Jefferson, Maryland, about eight miles west of Frederick on September fourteenth:

> We reached camp again about 10 o'clock at night, and found awaiting us marching orders for 2 o'clock the following morning. Late as it was, one of my tent-mates—an enterprising young fellow—started out on a foraging expedition, in pursuance of a vow made several days before to find something with which to vary his monotonous regimen of "hard-tack" and "salt horse". He "ran the guard"—an easy thing to do in the darkness and hub-bub—and returned shortly after, struggling with a weight of miscellaneous plunder; a crock of butter, a quantity of apple-butter, some lard, a three-legged skillet weighing several pounds, and a live hen. It was a marvel how he carried [it all]...That night we had several immense flapjacks, the size of the whole pan; then, tethering the hen to one of the tent pegs, we went to sleep, to be roused an hour or so later by hearing our two-legged prize cackling and fluttering off in the darkness.

GOODBYE

A Minnesota private gives us these tragic images from his night on the battlefield of South Mountain:

> We camped there all night with the dead and dying all around us.
>
> The next morning I looked over the ground on our front and it was covered with the dead bodies of our enemies. There I saw a rebel sitting on a rock with a woman's picture in his hand as though he were looking at it, but he was dead.

SERGEANT FRENCH'S CONVERSATION

On the crest of South Mountain, through Fox's Gap, there was a stone wall on which sat a Confederate soldier. Passing by, Sergeant French, of the Sixth New Hampshire, approached the rebel and asked him what he wanted. Getting no answer, the sergeant moved closer.

"What does he want?" cried out another member of the Sixth. But by now, French realized why he hadn't answered. He was dead, killed instantly while climbing over the wall, a stake by his side holding him upright.

After this incident, the other New Hampshire boys used to kid French about his "trying to make a dead rebel talk."

LAST WORDS

Moving over South Mountain on the morning of the fifteenth, an Ohio Volunteer saw two dead Confederates lying under a projecting rock. "They had, most likely, crawled under there when wounded and then died. They lay as though they had been in conversation just before their death."

A "projecting rock" located alongside the old National Road at Turner's Gap. This could very possibly be the same rock referred to in the Ohio soldier's account. It can easily be seen today along what is now Alternate Route 40, on the western side of South Mountain.

THE BEST HIT

An amusing incident occurred the day after the Battle of South Mountain. As a regiment of "regulars" was passing to the front, a Massachusetts volunteer called out, "I don't see any difference in looks between regulars and volunteers."

To this, an "important looking" regular sergeant held up his shiny, impeccably maintained rifle, and shouted, "Here's where the difference comes in!"

Undaunted, the volunteer smiled coolly and called back, "Oh yes, we use *ours* to fight with."

The men considered this the best hit on South Mountain, "particularly when we took position between the regulars and rebels again as usual, before the next fighting occurred."

THE WELL

War is indiscriminate, and nowhere is this more apparent than in the aftermath of a terrible battle. As Mr. Henry Wise walked across his property on September 15, one can only imagine what must have been running through his mind. His once peaceful fields were now covered in every direction with dead and dying men. Troops, wagons, and

The Wise Farm, looking southeast, as it appeared just after the war.

Henry Wise's field as it looks today. The photo was taken from the position of the horse and buggy in the earlier photo.

horses were constantly moving up the road past his farmhouse. Surgeons were performing their horrific duties on moaning and crying patients, and burial details were digging into his precious farmland.

At one point that terrible morning, Mr. Wise learned that a group of Ohio soldiers had tired of digging and had simply dumped the bodies of several Confederate soldiers into his well. Hearing this, he immediately put a stop to it. Finally, however, realizing that his well had already been spoiled, and anxious to be rid of the bodies, he agreed with General Burnside to allow the bodies to be buried in his well, at the charge of a dollar a piece.

Fifty eight more rebel bodies were dumped in, filling the well to ground level.

A GIBE ABOUT SOAP

"War develops an infinite amount of wit and humor among soldiers," writes W.W. Blackford, an officer of J.E.B. Stuart's Confederate cavalry. "In every company there were aspirants for the honor of being the "funny man" of the command, whose study it was to get off good jokes." As the Confederates rode into the captured town of Harpers Ferry on September 15, the "funny men" took advantage of the opportunity:

> The men of the surrendered garrison, not having been exposed to the weather, were not at all sunburned, and this paleness to us at the time looked peculiar to soldiers, contrasting so strongly with our berry-brown complexions. As we marched along the street one of our troopers sang out to one of the men on the sidewalk, "I say, Yank, what sort of soap do you fellows use? It has washed all the color out of your faces," at which our side cheered. To this the man retorted, "Damn me, if you don't look like you had never used soap of any sort." Shouts of laughter greeted the reply from our men as well as the Yanks, and our man called back as he rode on, "Bully for you, Yank; you got me that time."

THE QUICK-THINKING CHAPLAIN

On Monday, September 15, members of the 3rd Maryland (Union) entered Boonsboro, a small town on the western side of South Mountain. The men had not eaten for some time and were extremely hungry. Seeing a little farmhouse at the foot of the mountain, the regiment's chaplain decided to ride over to see if he could "capture' a loaf or two of bread. Upon entering the kitchen he met the "good woman" of the house and asked if she had any bread he could buy. She said that she had only one loaf left, but finally agreed to sell it to him for one dollar. So the sale was made and the chaplain made his way outside with the loaf of bread under his arm.

Before he could mount his horse, however, he saw a Rebel approaching, carrying his gun in his hand. The chaplain did not panic but instead greeted the soldier and, not wearing a uniform, was taken as the "man of the house." The two men began talking about food and such and as they did, the soldier set his gun down. "My friend, that's a fine gun you have there," said the chaplain, casually putting his hand upon it.

"Yes. it is a fine piece," replied the unsuspecting Rebel.

The chaplain picked up the rifle and began admiring the smooth barrel. Then he quickly stepped back a few paces, leveled the gun at the Rebel and said, "You are my prisoner." "If ever a fellow on a foraging expedition was chop-fallen and bewildered, he was." The chaplain had his prisoner "about face" and then marched him back to the 3rd Maryland. The "Johnny" turned out to be a member of the 3rd South Carolina and a "gentleman of intelligence and ability—and was extremely mortified at the manner of his capture, by an unarmed chaplain."

The chaplain shared his supper with the South Carolinian and provided him with a good blanket as well as breakfast the next morning. The chaplain said that "altogether the fellow had a better time with me than he would of had 'out in the cold,' with his own troops, for, on taking leave of me... he heartily thanked me for my kindness, and we parted the best of friends."

THE BIG SPECULATION

One enterprising member of Stonewall Jackson's Corps tells how he turned a quick buck en route to Harpers Ferry:

> I made a big speculation at Williamsport; my messmates asked me to get some soda, as we needed it to make our biscuits. I went to a drug store to get it, asked the salesman for a pound, and the price was only eight cents. I gave him a Confederate note, which he took without hesitation, and gave me change. I then asked what he would sell a keg for; his reply, six cents per pound. I paid him at once, shouldered the keg, one hundred and twenty pounds, carried it to the river, where I induced a wagon to carry it to camp for me. I sold it that night for twenty-five cents per pound!

The Heartless Lieutenant

Passing through Boonsboro on the afternoon of the 15th, an Indiana soldier saw a group of Confederate prisoners under guard. Amongst the rebels was the man's brother, whom he had not seen or heard from for many years. The soldier approached his lieutenant, explained the situation, and asked permission to go talk to the man. The lieutenant replied with a "bluff refusal." The "moral" of the story: "very heartless men were occasionally found, even in the Union army."

Shopping

A member of Confederate General James Longstreet's command writes:

> We did some shopping in Hagerstown, devoting ourselves chiefly to the dry goods line, and bought waterproof cloth and some dress patterns to present to our lady friends in Richmond, where they were in great need of such things. One merchant had upon his top shelves about one hundred old-fashioned bell-crowned beaver hats, just the style our fathers wore. The store was soon relieved of the stock of beavers, and the streets were thronged with men with the new hats. They wore them upon the march, and went into the next battle with this most peculiar headgear for warriors.

After retreating from South Mountain, Lee selected a place to collect his scattered army and brazenly make a stand while still in Maryland. He chose the quiet little town of Sharpsburg. It would soon witness the bloodiest single day in American history.

PART III

CANNONADE AND BATTLE:
SEPTEMBER 16-17, 1862

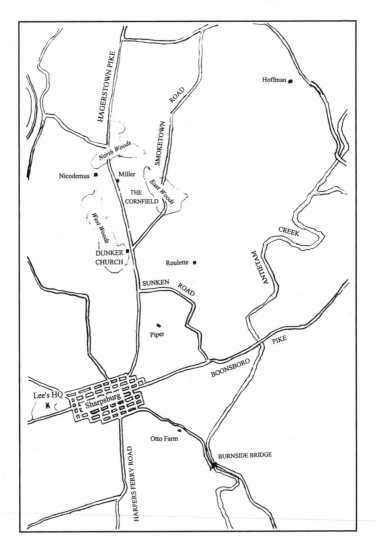

A Drink of Wine

When the Confederate army arrived at
Sharpsburg, General Longstreet set up his
headquarters at the fine farmhouse of Mr.
and Mrs. Henry Piper and their two young
daughters, just north of town. The Pip-
ers were pro-Union, but in spite of this,
the two girls offered Generals Longstreet
and D.H. Hill each a glass of wine from
their private stock. "Old Pete" Longstreet
politely declined, suspecting that the
drink may be poisoned. "Harvey" Hill,
graciously accepted their offer, however,
and began to drink. A few minutes
passed and Longstreet, seeing that Hill
hadn't dropped dead, turned to the Piper
girls and said, "Ladies, I will thank you
for a little of that wine."

*Major General
James Longstreet*

Brotherly Love

As General Joseph Hooker's First Corps moved through
Keedysville, a little town just to the east of Sharpsburg, on the sixteenth, the artillery boomed up the road ahead. A soldier in the ranks
relates this story.

"We'll have a tussle with them here," said a tall soldier who was
marching beside me.

"Yes," I replied, "but the Johnnies will find 'Little Mac' and Gen.
Hooker hard men to deal with."

A moment later my comrade spoke again. He was usually light-
hearted and merry, but now appeared strangely serious and thought-
ful. He had a brother in the company, and between the two men the
closest relations existed. The welfare of each other was their constant
thought. If rations were short, or duty bore more heavily on one than
upon the other, the rest of the company were given an illustration of
brotherly love which always had its good effect.

My comrade now looked around to make sure that his brother
should not hear him, and said, "George, I don't why it is, but I cannot
get over the feeling that I am to be hit in this fight. If I am, and you get
out all right, look out for Charley, won't you?"

"Certainly," said I, "but don't think anything like that is going to
happen. Look on the bright side."

The next morning, in Miller's cornfield, the worried soldier was
mortally wounded by his brother's side.

HIDING PLACE

Before the battle, a group of Confederate officers were going from house to house seeking information from the local citizens as to river crossings over the Potomac. When they entered the home of Mr. William Logan, the Confederates found Mrs. Logan standing in a corner of the room. Satisfied that the man of the house was not at home, the officers turned around and went on their way. Little did they know, however, that Mr. Logan had been at home. In fact, he had been in the same room with them, safely hidden under Mrs. Logan's skirts!

DEFENDING THE FLAG

The town of Sharpsburg was predominantly pro-Union and the ladies of the town had made a large American flag out of material that the townspeople had bought. The flag was proudly displayed in front of a blacksmith's house in the center of town. Upon hearing that Lee had invaded Maryland and was fast approaching, the blacksmith asked his twenty-year old daughter, "What you goin' to do with that flag? If the Rebels come into town they'll take it sure as the world."

He then suggested that they hide it somewhere. So, the daughter and a friend put the flag in a strong wooden box and buried it in the ash pile behind the smokehouse. On Sunday, the first of the Rebel cavalry rode into town. On Monday, more Confederates arrived and by evening the citizens knew that something big was going to happen.

This photo of Sharpsburg, taken two days after the battle, shows Main Street leading into town from the east.

Courtesy of William A. Frassanito, *Antietam: The Photographic Legacy of America's Bloodiest Day.*

Somehow, word had gotten to the Confederates that a Union flag was concealed at the blacksmith's house. Early Tuesday, three Rebels approached the house and were met at the door by the daughter. One of the soldiers spoke up sharply, "We've come to demand that flag you've got here. Give it up at once or we'll search the house."

The daughter was not frightened by the rough looking Rebels and replied, "I'll not give it up, and I guess you'll not come any farther than you are, sir." "If you don't tell me where that flag is I'll draw my revolver on you!," he warned her.

Still undaunted, the fiery woman answered, "It's of no use for you to threaten. Rather than have you touch a fold of that starry flag I laid it in the ashes." Thinking the flag destroyed, the Rebels moved on.

On Friday, after the Confederate army had retreated, the defiant Sharpsburg woman retrieved her beloved flag and once again it fluttered over the main street of town. Standing on the steps of her father's house, she saw a group of Confederate prisoners being marched by. Among them were the three men who had demanded the flag three days earlier. Seeing the flag, they became enraged and called out to her, "You said it was burned! We'll settle with you when we come back!"

But they never came back.

THEM BURSTING LAMP-POSTS

A "green" Confederate soldier described the shelling of Sharpsburg that took place during the artillery bombardment of September 16:

> Every shell went screaming, whistling, whining over our heads, and not a few burst near by us. Sometimes shell after shell would burst in quick succession over the village.... None of our soldiers were in the town, except the cooks and a few stragglers who hid themselves in the cellars as soon as the bombardment began, and told us afterwards of the wonderful escapes they made from 'them bursting lamp-posts.'

TO CATCH A THIEF

Many years after the battle, a former slave who lived at the Otto Farm on the Lower Bridge Road in Sharpsburg, remembered his own adventure on the day before the battle:

> On Tuesday all the Otto family left and went down country for safety. I stayed on the place. Once I fastened up the house tight and walked up in the field. By and by I had a feelin' that I'd better go back, and I went. I found someone

31

had broke a pane of glass in a window and reached in and took out the nail that kept the sash down. Then he'd raised the window and crawled in. Close by, inside of the room, was a washbench, and he'd set a crock of preserves and a crock of flour on it ready to carry away. I took the things and put 'em where they belonged and started on the trail of the thief. It was easy follerin' him, for he left all the doors open which he went through. In the dining room he'd poured out a lot of sugar on a handkercher to take along, and he'd gone into my old boss's room and strewed his papers around over the floor. Next he'd gone upsteps, and I went up 'em too, and hyar he was in a little pantry. He was a Rebel soldier—a young feller—and not very large. I was skeered, but he was mo' skeered than I was—certainly he was; and I said, "You dirty houn' you, I have a notion to take you and throw you down those steps."

Oh! I could have mashed him, for I saw he had no revolver. He didn't say anything. He left. I reckon I was too big for him.

THE DOG

During the cannonade, "a fine, large, shaggy, black dog was running about. The rebel shells would come over the top of the ridge behind which the regiment lay...This dog began fooling with the shells as they struck in the earth, burying themselves several inches. Soon, while the dog's paws and nose were pressing into the earth, just where one had entered, it exploded, sending a cloud of earth and dog into the air. The nose and lower jaw of the dog were blown away by the explosion, but he lived and ran about for some time."

NOT A BASEBALL

Charles Carleton Coffin was an army correspondent and was one of the first reporters on the scene at Antietam, arriving just after the outbreak of firing. From his writings we get many vivid pictures of the battle and its aftermath. Among the most curious is the image of a rolling, but still dangerous, cannonball. This incident took place just north of Miller's Cornfield.

I recall a round shot that came ricocheting over the ground, cutting little furrows, tossing earth into the air, as the plow of a locomotive turns its white furrow after a snowstorm. Its speed gradually diminished and a soldier was about to catch it, as if

32

he were at a game of baseball, but a united yell of "look out!" "Don't!" "Take care!" "Hold on!" caused him to desist. Had he attempted it, he would have been knocked over instantly.

STRANGE MISSILES AT ANTIETAM

It was a common rumor throughout the Union ranks at Antietam that the Confederate artillerists used other items beside standard ordnance in their guns. Although the validity of this is questionable at best, this story is worth repeating.

Broken railroad iron and blacksmith's tools, hammers, chisels, &c., were fired from rebel cannon. Some of these missiles made a peculiar noise, resembling "which away, which away" by which the national troops came to distinguish them from the regular shot and shell, and as they heard them approaching would cry, "Turkey! turkey coming!" and fall flat to avoid them. An artillerist, a German, when he saw the tools falling around him, exclaimed, "My Got! We shall have the blacksmiths's shop come next!"

RATIONS

Late on the afternoon of the sixteenth, as the thunder of artillery filled the air, a regiment of Delaware soldiers lounged about a Federal commissary waiting out the storm. One of the men was sitting on a barrel of beans when suddenly a stray cannonball came out of nowhere and smashed the barrel to smithereens. The soldier, miraculously unharmed, picked himself up, began brushing himself off, and coolly walked away, saying, "If that's the way rations are served around here, I'm not hungry at all. Thank you."

RUNNING FOR COVER

As the air around them howled and screamed during the artillery duel of the sixteenth, members of the Confederate Rockbridge Artillery saw an "unusually large" man equipped with a sword at his side come running across the field at a full sprint. A few yards to the rear the burly man leaped over and immediately hid behind a large log. He had only been there a moment when the log was smashed by a cannon ball. The stunned man then "reappeared as part of the upheaval; but, regaining his feet, broke for the woods with the speed of a quarterhorse, and a greater confidence in distance than in logs."

BREAKFAST IS INTERRUPTED

A slave woman, who was a cook at a tavern in Sharpsburg, relates this incident. It is amazing to think how close the Confederacy came to losing their cherished military leader, and how differently the course of the war might have run.

> General Lee come to the house early the next morning [the 17th]. He was a fine-lookin' man, and he was the head general of 'em all in the Rebel army, you know. Our old boss was a Democrat, too; so he gave the general his breakfast. But while the officers was eatin' there in the dining room a shell come right thoo the wall and busted and scattered brick and daubin' all over everything. There was so much dirt you couldn't tell what was on the table. I was bringin' in coffee from the kitchen and had a cup and saucer in my hand. I don't know where I put that coffee, but I throwed it away, and we all got out of there in a hurry.

CHAOS IN THE STREETS

The slave woman in the aforementioned story also gives us this view of the pandemonium that enveloped the usually sleepy, little town of Sharpsburg:

> By and by word was sent in for the women and children to all leave town. That was about—le's see—between ten and 'leven o'clock, I reckon. We went out on the street, and there lay a horse with his whole backbone split wide open. The ambulances was comin' into town, and the wounded men in 'em was hollerin,' "O Lord! O Lord! O Lord!"
>
> Poor souls! and the blood was runnin' down thoo the bottom of the wagons. Some of the houses was hospitals, and the doctors was cuttin' off people's legs and arms and throwin' 'em out the do' jest like throwin' out old sticks.
>
> We hadn't gone only a couple of houses when a shell busted right over our heads. So we took back to the cellar in a hurry. The way they was shootin' and goin' on we might have been killed befo' we was out of town.

UPSETTING SHOT

The morning of the battle, a Federal soldier was seated on his knapsack, facing the rear. Suddenly, "a shell fired at the battery on the hill in front of us struck the ground, bounded and struck the ground just back of me,... plowed a hole under me from back to front and came out between my feet. The ground settled down into the trench, my knapsack and I going down with it. Well, that shell was given room as quickly as possible. I rolled over three or four times and the other boys who were sitting near did the same, but fortunately it did not burst and no one got more than a good start.

"MOTHER HUBBARDS"

A member of General J.E.B. Stuart's cavalry was near Nicodemus Hill as Pelham's Confederate battery was engaged in a duel with Federal artillery to the northwest of this position. Between the opposing forces was the Nicodemus Farmhouse where a number of civilians had taken refuge. The Rebel cavalryman wrote:

> When the crossing shells began screaming over the house, its occupants thought their time had come, and like a flock of birds they came streaming out in 'Mother Hubbards,'...hair streaming in the wind and children of all ages stretched out behind, and tumbling at every step over the clods of ploughed fields. Every time one would fall, the rest thought it was the result of a cannon shot and ran the faster. It was impossible to keep from laughing at this sudden eruption and impossible to persuade them to return.

The Confederate then rode out to the frightened party and tried to convince them to go back to the house. The group, however, could not be persuaded. So, the cavalryman scooped up as many children as his horse could carry and led them back to his lines. Seeing what was happening, both sides ceased firing until the civilians were out of danger.

NO RESPECT

While engaged in horrific combat near the Dunker Church, members of the Confederate "Rockbridge Artillery" quickly became annoyed by the antics of a young, newly commissioned lieutenant who had previously been a lowly orderly at brigade headquarters.

Feeling his newly acquired importance, he spurred his horse around among the guns, calling out, "Let 'em have it!" and the like, until, seeing our disgust at his impertinent encouragement, and that we preferred a chance to let him have it, he departed.

The Dunker Church

LUNCH MEAT

Early in the morning of the seventeenth the battle opened about a mile north of the Dunker Church. During the early stages of the fighting, the members of the 21st New York found themselves just west of the Hagerstown Pike in the grass fields of the Nicodemus family.

Amidst the chaotic din of battle the men heard the agonized squeals of a fat pig which had been hit by a stray shot. Despite all the excitement and danger of the situation, one soldier had his mind on the potential of a nice, hearty pork lunch. So, dropping his rifle he left the ranks and rushed to the pig. Drawing his sheath knife and "with the practical hand of a professional butcher brings the lingering sickness of Mr. Pig to an abrupt termination." After rolling the pig into a ditch to hide it the soldier ran back and took his place in line.

Stonewall's Tree-Top Scout

General "Stonewall" Jackson was standing with General John Bell Hood in the woods behind the Dunker Church. He turned to Hood and told him to find a good climber to go up a tree and ascertain the strength of the Union Army advancing from the North and East Woods. Hood soon selected a 16 year old boy from the 35th North Carolina by the name of Clark [probably adjutant Walter Clark]. In no time Clark was perched atop a nearby tree, peering off into the northeast at the masses of blue uniforms.

"How's it look?" asked Jackson.

Clark looked down and said, "There's oceans of 'em Gen'ral."

"Never mind the oceans. Count the battle flags."

Clark began to count out loud and when he reached 37 Jackson said, "That will do; come down and we will get out of here."

Lieutenant White

The story of William Greenough White, a first lieutenant in Hooker's Corps, is an amazing one. While still battling a vicious fever, White left his hospital bed and managed to rejoin his outfit just hours before the commencement of the battle. The soldiers were ecstatic to see their beloved commander.

The brave lieutenant could not stand to see his boys go into a fight without him and on the morning of the seventeenth he led them into The Cornfield. Soon after, the firing began and a piece of shrapnel hit White in the foot and tore off two toes. A major "advises him to go to the rear, but he only smiles and says he is 'worth a dozen dead men yet.'"

The regiment advanced further over that terrible ground with the brave lieutenant limping along in the face of the enemy. Again he was asked to go to the rear but, raising himself to his full height, he replied, "somewhat scornfully: 'I shall not leave my company.'"

A soldier who was there described what happened next:

> Lieutenant White remains still. His eyes glow with the joy of battle, and he seems to be everywhere imparting courage and stimulating the efforts of his men. By-and-by he is struck again. A piece of shell has stripped the flesh from the upper part of one of his arms. The shock is severe enough to throw him to the ground, but he quickly rises again and his voice is heard...above the din of battle. I look at his face to see if he shows evidences of pain and am met with a cheery smile. By this time our ranks have become fearfully decimated, and the Lieutenant begins moving those who are yet in line up nearer the colors. "Let us die under the flag boys!" he cries.

The lieutenant was hit a third time. His hip was shattered and his abdomen "torn open in a shocking manner." Above the hellish noise and chaos White was heard yelling to his men, "Don't mind me; give it to them!"

The same soldier continued the narration:

> At last we reach Poffenberger's and lay our dying friend at Surgeon Hayward's feet. The doctor examines his wounds. The Lieutenant talks lightly of his hurts, and with his own hands replaces the torn flesh. This exhibition of heroism is too much even for professional self-control, and the surgeon turns aside and bursts into tears.
>
> ...Those who were with him when he died told us he was brave to the last. He died late in the afternoon. One of his lower limbs was very painful just before he breathed his last. An attendant was rubbing it. "Does this rubbing do you any good Lieutenant?" "No," he said, "but that cheering does," for just then our troops had gained an advantage.

CLOSE CALLS

A Union private of Lieutenant White's company gives a vivid account of his own harrowing experiences in the fighting near the Cornfield:

> My ramrod is wrenched from my grasp as I am about to return it to its socket after loading. I look for it behind me, and the Lieutenant passes me another, pointing to my own, which lies bent and unfit for use across the face of a dead man. A bullet enters my knapsack just under my left arm while I am taking aim. Another passes through my haversack, which hangs upon my left hip. Still another cuts both strings of my canteen, and that useful article joins the debris now thickly covering the ground. Having lost all natural feeling I laugh at these mishaps as though they were huge jokes, and remark to my nearest neighbor that I shall soon be relieved of all my trappings. A man but a few paces from me is struck squarely in the face by a solid shot. Fragments of the poor fellow's head come crashing into my face and fill me with disgust. I grumble about it as though it wa' something that might have been avoided.

THE DISGUISE

In an area near the East Woods, as the 13th New Jersey came under fire, someone in the ranks asked what had become of John Ick and Reddy Mahar, two members of their company. Lem Smith, another member of the company, said that he saw them heading towards the rear at a run. Sergeant Hank Van Orden was then ordered to go find the two and bring them back. Off he went and before long he came to a tree at the base of which was a large rock. But as the sergeant moved closer, the rock started to look a little odd. Suddenly, the "rock" coughed. Van Orden gave the rock a swift kick and up popped John Ick. He had found an old, mud covered, rubber overcoat and drawn it over him. But now the jig was up and the sergeant ordered the skulker back to the regiment. Ick said that he had "had enough of the slaughter house business and was going home." The sergeant had no patience for this, however, and made him come along. In the end, though, Ick got over his panic and performed well in battle.

CAPTAIN BACHELLE'S DOG

Union Major R. R. Dawes, whose 6th Wisconsin was involved in the vicious fighting of the Cornfield, gives us this sad tale:

Captain Bachelle had a fine Newfoundland dog, which had been trained to perform military salutes and many other remarkable things. In camp, on the march, and in the line of battle, the dog was his constant companion. The dog was by his side when he fell. Our line of men left the body when they retreated, but the dog stayed with his dead master, and was found on the morning of the 19th of September, lying dead upon his body.

THE UNARMED SERGEANT

Preparing to charge into the area of the Cornfield, the 12th Massachusetts formed its line of battle. Suddenly, a sergeant of Company G, whom they had left in Washington, appeared on the scene. "Captain, can't I take my place in line?" he pleaded.

To this the surprised captain retorted, "Why, sergeant! Where did you come from?"

"Oh! They brought me to Frederick, and I slipped away from there."

"Well, but you have no rifle."

"Yes. But I can soon raise one."

"Go in, then."

The unarmed sergeant went into battle with his men. Before long "a canister-shot crashes through the brain of a man in Company C and our watchful sergeant pounces on him like an eagle on his prey, tears the rifle from his dying grasp, and triumphantly rejoins his company."

BATTERY HORSES

During the fighting north of the Dunker Church, a Confederate soldier was witness to this terrible, almost surreal-like scene:

> ...I saw a horse galloping...dragging something. Thinking it was his rider as he emerged from the clouds of smoke on the field of battle, I moved to intercept and stop the animal, but to my horror discovered that the horse was dragging his own entrails from the gaping wound of a cannonball, and after passing us a few yards the poor brute fell dead with a piercing scream. The wounded horses of a battery will stay around their mates as long as the battery is in action and then try to follow, whatever their condition may be.

Another tragic testimonial to this desperate loyalty comes from a member of the Rockbridge Artillery who saw a battery horse lose a leg during the fighting. After transferring his harness to another horse, the team took off at a trot. Seeing this, "the crippled horse took his place close by where he was accustomed to work, and kept alongside on three legs until his suffering was relieved by a bullet in the brain.

A SOLDIER STAGGERS

"At the battle of Antietam, as one of the regiments was for the second time going into the conflict, a soldier staggered. It was from no wound, but in the group of dying and dead through which they were passing, he saw his father, of another regiment, lying dead. A wounded man, who knew them both, pointed to the father's corpse, and then upwards, saying only, 'It is all right with him.' Onward went the son, by his father's corpse, to do his duty in the line, which, with bayonets fixed, advanced upon the enemy. When the battle was over, he came back, and with other help, buried his father. From his person he took the only thing he had, a Bible, given to the father years before, when he was an apprentice."

THE SKEDADDLER

Edmund Brown, a member of the 27th Indiana, was standing with his troops in the North Woods before the regiment advanced towards

The Cornfield. The gravity of the moment was, for a time, lightened by the humorous antics of a "skedaddler."

Upon the higher ground to our right, one lone, panicked skedadler runs by. Judge of the character of the troops in our front when the fact is stated, and it is a fact, that this was the only able-bodied soldier we saw running out of the fight! This one is in a cornfield and runs zig-zag among the corn, dodging frantically from one hill across to another in the opposite row, as if trying to escape from a swarm of bees. At the sound of a passing shell he throws himself upon the ground and remains motionless, with his nose rooted in the soil, while the shell goes a mile. This is the more ludicrous to us because we can see the shell, and can see plainly that, besides having passed him before he fell down, it had missed him by a wide margin anyway. Eventually he jumps to his feet and runs as before. While the boys laugh, they also guy him unmercifully, heaping upon him epithets far more true than complimentary. But nothing stops him.

This picture was taken from the position of the 27th Indiana before its advance toward The Cornfield. At the time of the battle, it was the most easterly portion of the North Woods. The "skedadler" was seen running from left to right along the high ground to the right of the photograph.

A BRAVE MAN

During the attack near the Dunker Church, this curious incident occurred in the ranks of the Nineteenth Massachusetts.

While descending this slope, Ernest A. Nichols, of Company C, a lad of but 17, was hit by a spent ball on the breast plate and fell forward. Someone said "Nichols is gone" but he sprang up again and took his place in the ranks, saying, "I'm not killed yet." Major Rice heard his remark and responded, "There's a brave man."

THE BAYONET

Throughout the Civil War, men of both sides carried with them that imposing-looking instrument of war known as the bayonet. They soon found out, however, that they were more useful as candle holders or cooking tools than as weapons. Because of the vastly improved technology, chiefly the rifle musket, troops rarely got close enough to one another to use the bayonet. It did happen on occasion, though, and from the diary of a Union Army Surgeon we get this sad tale, proof of the brutal nature of the fighting in that area known simply as "The Cornfield."

"Lieutenant Haskell, of General Gibbon's staff, while riding in the cornfield, returning from delivering an order, came across a corporal in the Second Wisconsin regiment. The corporal was badly wounded. The lieutenant asked him how he came by such an ugly wound in his breast. 'Was it a piece of shell that hit you?' The dying corporal feebly replied, 'No, I was wounded first by a musket-ball, and afterwards a rebel thrust a bayonet into my breast.'"

BROTHER BEFRIENDS BROTHER

Sergeant Sam Bloomer, the color bearer of the 1st Minnesota, had his right knee shattered while at the rail fence along the Hagerstown Pike. Seeking shelter, he crawled into the West Woods near the Dunker Church. When Sedgwick's Division was driven from the field, Sergeant Bloomer was left there. Some members of the First Georgia Regulars, of "Tige" Anderson's Brigade who had been sent to assist General Hood, found the wounded sergeant lying at the base of a tree in great pain. Feeling for their wounded enemy, First Sergeant W.H. Andrews, along with several other Georgians, assisted the helpless Yankee by piling up cordwood in front of him to shield him from the bullets.

After the battle, Sergeant Bloomer had his wounded leg amputated at the David Hoffman barn, on the battlefield. He survived the operation. Forty years later, Sam Bloomer still remained in touch with W.H. Andrews, the Georgia soldier who had shown him kindness on that awful September day back in 1862.

The Feeling of a Wound

What is it like to be wounded in battle? Most of us, fortunately, will never know. But, through this account by a soldier of the 57th New York, some insight is gained into one particular experience.

It was in the heat of the battle that a shell burst almost over his head and he was struck with a fragment of it in the right side of the neck and shoulder. It was not painful, he says, but produced rather a pleasant sensation as though he was flying through the air. This was due to the benumbing feeling that comes with such a wound. He could not tell what had happened to him, but after a while felt as though there was a hole through his forehead. Then came a feeling that he was about killed and must die. Several sinking spells followed, he thought of his mother and prayed to the Lord to have mercy on him, and then again he faints, and again revives and feels for the hole in his head. He looks around and asks a comrade where he is hit. "Half of the neck and part of the head is torn away," is the response. He begs to be taken off the field so as not to be captured by the enemy and is carried to the little school house in the apple orchard and thence to a barn [Roulette], where he lay two nights and three days on a wad of hay with the blue sky for his covering...It is one of the strange things of the war that this comrade, seemingly so fatally wounded, is yet living, though crippled.

Religion Under Fire

Religion was a vital factor in the lives of many soldiers in the Civil War, none more so than members of the predominantly Catholic Irish Brigade. William Corby, the brigade's chaplain, spurred his horse to the front of the line as the men were charging the Sunken Road. As he remembered, "I had only time to wheel my horse for an instant toward them and gave my poor men a hasty absolution...In twenty or thirty minutes after this absolution, 506 of these very men lay on the field, either dead or seriously wounded." Then, amidst a hail of bullets, the Chaplain dismounted and began hearing the confessions of the fallen. Miraculously, he survived the ordeal unharmed, and no doubt comforted many souls in their dying moments.

Cheering the Boys Up

A member of the 19th Massachusetts relates this tale, contrasting the horrors of battle with the grit and humor of the common soldier.

Captain Hale received a very peculiar wound. A minie ball carried away all his front teeth and a piece of his tongue, making a painful and disabling wound. Sergt. McGinnis, who had received a bullet wound in the breast, saw Capt. Hale as he sat in the temporary hospital, his lips swelled so that he could hardly open them and his face puffed out, trying to drink some tea. Thinking to "cheer the boys up a bit," he said to the wounded officer, "Oh, Captain, how I'd just like to kiss you now." The poor Captain could not laugh as it hurt his lips to move them, and could only sputter in his pain. Sergt. McGinnis then lay upon the operating table and had his bullet removed without taking anesthetics.

NINE AND TEN

During the height of the battle, the 9th Massachusetts was marching down a road behind Union lines. From the opposite direction on the same road came another regiment from the Bay State—the 10th Massachusetts. As the two regiments passed and realized the amazing irony of the situation, they began cheering and calling out, "Hello Ninth!" and, "Hello Tenth!"

Then one "droll fellow" of the Ninth called out, "I say, Tenth, as you're the last out, have you any letters for us?" The men burst out in laughter and as they did the other regiments around them began "wondering what so much cheering and laughing was about, anyway."

MOTHER AND CHILD

During the battle, most citizens of Sharpsburg retreated to their basements for safety. In the large cellar of the Kretzer House [still standing today at 128 East Main St.] 200 hundred people of all ages huddled together in darkness, as their peaceful town was enveloped by the sounds of war. Among them was Mrs. Henry Ward who was holding a baby in her arms, born only days earlier. Her condition was still weak from the birthing process and, fearing for her own and her baby's health in the damp, cool basement, some men carried her upstairs. She had only been there a short time when there was a loud explosion, followed by a massive cloud of dust, smoke, and debris, momentarily blinding the terrified mother and child. She pleaded not to be left upstairs with the shells falling so thickly in the town. So the men placed her in a big arm chair and brought her back down into the cellar.

Nervous Private Lloyd

Thomas Galwey, a Union volunteer from Ohio, was lying with his regiment in a cornfield near the Roulette House. Suddenly, a shell exploded nearby with a thundering crack, leaving Galwey permanently deaf in his right ear. A splinter of the same shell struck and wounded Private Joseph Lloyd. Galwey and three others lifted their wounded comrade and began carrying him back towards the Roulette barn. Suddenly, another shell exploded nearby sending hot shrapnel into both thighs of one of the party, a sergeant of the Seventh Ohio. The sergeant, his legs incapacitated, needed two men to carry him and Galwey was left to escort Private Lloyd off the field on his own.

The two men hobbled along as best they could until finally Galwey, utterly exhausted, turned to Lloyd and said he must rest. Lloyd, "at all times a nervous man, and now more so than ever, though his wound is slight," said they must go on. He told Galwey that it made little difference if he was killed, for he was a bachelor. If Lloyd were killed, however, his poor wife and children would be left destitute. Galwey remembered, "Stunned as I was from the frightful explosion that had deprived me of the use of an ear, and tired, hungry, and sad from the sight of so much carnage as I had seen during the day, I could not resist laughter at the combination of impudence and absurdity in Lloyd's remark."

The Roulette House, photographed just days after the battle.

Courtesy of William A. Frassanito, *Antietam: The Photographic Legacy of America's Bloodiest Day.*

No Fear

Approximately 100 yards in front of the Sunken Road, there is a drop-off in the ground. This incline provided attacking Union troops of the 2nd Corps some cover from the Confederate fire. It was here that members of the 132nd Pennsylvania found themselves on the afternoon of the seventeenth, using this embankment for protection while firing into what became known as Bloody Lane. During the "fiercest of the fighting" a strange, almost unbelievable incident occurred. Over the sounds of battle, the Pennsylvanians heard a man's voice calling out, "Come over here men, you can see 'em better." When the men looked over the brow of the knoll they saw Private George Coursen, of Company K, "sitting on a boulder, loading and firing as calmly as though there wasn't a rebel in the country." They yelled for him to come back behind the hill but he "said he could see the rebels better there, and refused to leave his vantage-ground." The private stayed there until the regiment was ordered back and never received so much as a scratch. "His escape was nothing less than a miracle" and "well illustrated the fortunes of war."

View looking northeast from just behind the Confederate position in the Sunken Road. The 132nd Pennsylvania was located just beyond the bluff toward the right of the picture.

DEADLY MERCY

In the following story, a man's compassion for an enemy led to his own death. It happened near the Sunken Road.

...A rebel soldier was seen approaching with a limping gait, using his musket as a support. Sergeant Dunn raised his musket, saying, "I'll drop that fellow." Before he could fire, his piece was struck down by Captain Rickards, who exclaimed, "You wouldn't shoot a wounded man!" At that instant the advancing rebel leveled his gun and shot Captain Rickards, who died a few minutes afterwards. The dastard rebel then fell dead in his tracks, riddled with bullets.

FATHER AND SON

During the height of battle, Confederate General John B. Gordon found an older man, lying mortally wounded, beside the body of his dead son. The "grey-haired hero" called out to the general, "Here we are. My boy is dead, and I shall go soon. But it is all right."

HOT SEAT

Members of the 8th Ohio saw, for a fleeting instant amidst the battle smoke, a Confederate running on an exposed portion of ground just behind the Sunken Road. After the fighting, a member of the regiment walked over this part of the field and found the "poor fellow...his rear parts full of lead!"

THE PICK-POCKET

A Union soldier attacking the Rebels entrenched in the Sunken Road tells of this interesting episode:

At length the Irish Brigade came into close touch with us, an orderly sergeant kneeling down, I remember, just at my left shoulder and banging away at the enemy. He was a redheaded, red-bearded man, and the whole circumstance is impressed on my mind from the fact that he put his hand into the haversack of a dead Confederate and took therefrom a bag of coffee, which he kept for himself, handing to me a bag of sugar.

"I KNEW I WAS GONE"

To Union Lieutenant A. H. Nickerson it seemed as if everyone around him had been killed as he battled in front of the Sunken Road. A small boy named Johnny stood by him, handing him cartridges, in spite of the fact that his arm had been shattered by a bullet. As the lieutenant rammed down the last available cartridge, he heard the whir of a bullet pass close by and strike a small tree just behind him. Looking up, he saw a tall Confederate slowly lower his gun and then drop down behind the embankment to reload. The top of the Reb's hat was still visible and with his last round Lieutenant Nickerson drew a careful bead and squeezed the trigger. He missed.

The Rebel's head now popped up. Nickerson turned to Johnny only to find him gone. A dead soldier lay at the lieutenant's feet and from his cartridge box he quickly grabbed a round, "bit off the end, poured in the powder, and forced the bullet in." The bullet, however, was defective, and became jammed halfway down the barrel. As Nickerson frantically tried to ram the ball into his gun, his Rebel adversary stood up, slowly leveled his rifle, and took careful aim. At this point the lieutenant said, "I knew I was gone." The Reb fired and Nickerson "felt the sharp jab of the bullet, a blur about the eyes, and the warm blood running down my right side as that arm fell helpless." The bullet had passed through the shoulder and exited without hitting the bone. The lieutenant was extremely lucky that terrible day.

REBEL TARGET

Near the Sunken Road, a Confederate soldier was killed while in the act of climbing over a rock. He remained in a life-like position with his hand and arm extended. Throughout the rest of the fighting he continued to draw the attention of the Union troops and when his body was found after the battle, it was "literally riddled with bullets— there must have been hundreds—and most of them shot into him after he was dead, for they showed no marks of blood."

WAR PAINT

When the Rebels were finally driven from the Sunken Road, Union troops quickly occupied this strategic location and continued to pour fire on the fleeing Confederates. Thomas Livermore, a member of the 5th New Hampshire, relates the madness and fury of the fighting here:

As the fight grew furious, the colonel cried out, "Put on the war paint" and looking around I saw the glorious man standing erect, with a red handkerchief, a conspicuous mark, tied around his bare head and the blood from some wounds on his forehead streaming over his face, which was blackened with powder. Taking the cue somehow we rubbed the torn end of the cartridges over our faces, streaking them with powder like a pack of Indians, and the colonel, to complete the similarity, cried out, "Give 'em the war whoop!" and all of us joined him in the Indian war whoop until it must have rung out above all the thunder of the ordnance. I have sometimes thought it helped to repel the enemy by alarming him to see this devilish-looking line of faces, and hear the horrid whoop; and at any rate, it reanimated us and let him know we were unterrified.

In a Pinch

A Union soldier in the Bloody Lane, finding himself without a weapon, used some gruesome ingenuity.

> The dead rebel whom I knelt on held in his hands a "Belgian rifle" (a poor enough arm, but worth something in a pinch like this), ...the cap on this rifle denoted that it was loaded, I took it out of his hands, and discharged it at his living comrades, and liking the work I looked around for another piece to discharge.

Grisly Sight

> "In the depth of the (Sunken) lane, where I stooped to give a wounded Southerner a drink of water from my canteen, I saw a Confederate captain with both eyes shot out. He was still alive and groaning!"

Brave Yankee "Rascal"

From the recollections of an Alabama officer comes this amazing story of bravery and coolness under fire. It happened on the Piper Farm as the Confederates were driving the Federal troops back towards the Sunken Road.

> When the enemy were scurrying back...over the hill which was to give them protection, they were completely demoralized; very few used their muskets as they retreated, but there was one man who never marched out of common-time. He marched as deliberately as if on drill...loading while going eight or ten steps, then turning and firing. Again and again he fired as he went up the hill and when he got to the top, all his comrades being out of sight...he fired for the last time, and then, turning, he slapped his hand on his posterior, to indicate the contempt in which he had us...
>
> While he was walking up that hillside alone, firing at us and his balls were whistling close by, I shouted to my men, "I will give the man a furlough that will shoot that rascal!" At that time I meant business. The bravest of the enemy were the men I wanted to kill—they set bad examples, and that was no time for sentiment.

BLOODY LANE

Of all of the scenes of carnage on any Civil War battlefield, the Sunken Road or "Bloody Lane" as it came to be known, was among the worst. This natural fortification soon became a slaughter pen as men of Richardson's Division of the Union Second Corps began raking it with fire. The Rebel casualties were staggering in this small stretch of farm lane. Reporter Charles Carleton Coffin describes the sight here just after the battle:

> What a ghastly spectacle!...Words are inadequate to portray the scene. Resolution and energy still lingered in the pallid cheeks, in the set teeth, in the gripping hand. I recall a soldier with the cartridge between his thumb and forefinger, the end of the cartridge bitten off, and the paper between his teeth when the bullet had pierced his heart, and the machinery of life—all the muscles and nerves—had come to a standstill. A young lieutenant had fallen while trying to rally his men: his hand still firmly grasping his sword, and determination was visible in every line of his face. I counted fourteen bodies lying together, literally in a heap, amid the corn rows on the hillside. The broad, green leaves were sprinkled and stained with blood.

Just two days after the battle, photographer Alexander Gardner arrived at the Antietam Battlefield. This was one of the images he captured. The Sunken Road would from now on be called Bloody Lane. These men were from North Carolina.

Bloody Lane as it appears today.

A SHOT FOR HILL

During the battle Generals Lee, Longstreet, and D. H. Hill were observing Federal positions from atop a hill near the citizens' cemetery which provided a good vantage point. Lee and Longstreet dismounted from their horses but the stubborn Hill would not. Longstreet provides the narrative:

> I said to Hill, "If you insist on riding up there and drawing the fire, give us a little interval so that we may not be in the line of fire when they open on you." General Lee and I stood on top of the crest with our glasses...After a moment I turned my glass to the right—the Federal left. As I did so I noticed a puff of white smoke from the mouth of a cannon. "There is a shot for you," I said to General Hill. The gunner was a mile away, and the cannon-shot came whisking through the air for three or four seconds and took off the front legs of the horse that Hill sat on and let the animal down upon his stumps. The horse's head was so low and his croup so high that Hill was in a most ludicrous position. With one foot in the stirrup he made several efforts to get the other leg over the croup, but failed. Finally we prevailed upon him to try the other end of the horse, and he got down.

The Can

A short time before the battle, a Federal soldier received a can of honey from home. When the honey was eaten a young recruit begged him for the empty can. Although thinking this a strange request, the soldier consented and gave him the can.

During a lull in the fighting of the seventeenth, the men "indulged in what had now become a chronic pastime—cooking." A soldier who was there tells what happened next:

> Soon there was a rousing fire...[and] the choice places along the line of flaming rails were in a few minutes, covered with black coffee cups—among them the new, *bright honey can*, with the lid screwed down. The recruit was chuckling to himself, while watching the pot, that he would have his coffee first, when alas! through his lack of knowledge of the expansive force of steam, this innocent man came near blowing his own head off, and scalding the whole company.
>
> He stood over his patent coffee-pot to see how near done his coffee was when, whi-z-z-z! bang!! and up went the can like a rocket into the air, tearing the fire to pieces, scattering rails and cups in every direction... How that recruit did get roundly cursed for his thick-headed stupidity, nor were the old grumblers satisfied, or their anger cooled off, until this bungler had filled all of the canteens again, and once more started the coffee cups on their bubbling rounds.

Poor Reb

A scowling Rebel was passing by General Lee's headquarters in town when he was stopped by the general himself. Lee asked the man where he was going.

"Goin to the rear," he grimly responded.

"And leave your comrades and your flag at such a time?" asked General Lee.

"Look'ee here, General, I've been stunted by a bung and I'm a leetle the durndest demoralized Reb you ever seen!"

"Let him go," said the General, and the doleful soldier trampled on his way.

A Dreadful Spectacle

David Thompson of the Ninth New York Volunteers recalls this bizarre incident which occurred near Burnside's Bridge:

I saw... a rolled overcoat with its straps on bound into the air and fall among the furrows. One of the enemy's grapeshot had plowed a groove in the skull of a young fellow and had cut his overcoat from his shoulders. He never stirred from his position, but lay there face downward—a dreadful spectacle.

WISE-CRACKING "TAR HEEL"

A captured North Carolina soldier, a member of Stonewall Jackson's command, was being led to the Union rear the afternoon of the sixteenth. Apparently, he was quite a character and greatly amused his captors. At one point the "dull-looking Tar Heel" stepped off the road to examine several pieces of artillery which were parked. At each cannon he read aloud "U.S.," which was printed on the barrel of every gun.

"Well what now, Johnny Reb?" asked one of his good-natured escorts.

"I say, Mister," replied the Reb, "you-all has got most as many of these U.S. guns as we'uns has."

Everyone around exploded in laughter "as the discomfited guard hurried 'Johnny' to the rear."

BRAVE MISS MILLER

From the memoirs of Henry Kyd Douglas, a member of Stonewall Jackson's staff, comes this amazing story of a Sharpsburg citizen:

> I was crossing the main street of town...when I saw a young lady, Miss Savilla Miller, whom I knew, standing on the porch of her father's house, as if unconscious of the danger she was in. At that time the firing was very heavy, and ever anon a shell would explode over the town or in the streets, breaking windows, knocking down chimneys, perforating houses and roofs. Otherwise the village was quiet and deserted, as if it was given up to ruin. It gave one an odd sensation to witness it. Knowing the great danger to which Miss Savilla was exposed, I rode up to protest and ask her to leave.
>
> "I will remain here as long as our army is between me and the Yankees," she replied with a calm voice, although there was excitement in her face. "Won't you have a glass of water?"
>
> Before I had time to answer, she was gone with her pitcher to the well and in an instant she was back again with a glass in her hand. As she approached me...a shell with a shriek in its

flight came over the hill, passed just over us down the street and exploded not far off. My horse, "Ashby," sank so low in his fright that my foot nearly touched the curb, some cowardly stragglers on the other side of the street, trying to hide behind a low porch, pressed closer to the foundations of the house, but over the face of the heroic girl only a faint shadow passed. She poured out the cooling drink and handed it to me without a word of fear or comment. Repeating my warning, I lifted my hat and went on my way to Dunker Church. She remained at her post all day. When a cannon shot and then a shell passed through the house from the gable, she took refuge for a little while in the cellar; but when the battle ended, she was still holding the fort.

FREAKS OF WAR

W. W. and J. H. Humphrey were brothers fighting in the same New Hampshire regiment. One was left-handed and the other was right-handed. In the battle of Antietam the left-handed one had his left thumb shot off and the right handed one lost his right thumb. "Such were the freaks of war."

THE RIDE

"As we were crossing the lane near the bridge (Burnside's), ...just as I reached the top rail of the fence I saw a sow, with her litter of pigs, come running up the bank from the creek. The poor thing was so frightened she didn't know which way to turn, and came rushing pell-mell through the ranks, catching one of the men between the legs and carrying him off astride her back, his rifle waving in the air and he shouting for help at the top of his voice. Without doubt both steed and rider were glad when the impromptu ride came to an end."

SCARED STIFF

After advancing up the bluff near Burnside's Bridge, the 9th New Hampshire was ordered to take a position along a rail fence. Suddenly, a soldier in the ranks dropped to the ground.

"Get up!" shouted his captain to him.

"I can't!" replied the man.

Finally the captain ordered a few men of the company to lay the man in a safe spot where he wouldn't be hit. The following day, when ranks were called, the soldier reported for duty. He had been "completely prostrated by nervous excitement" while under fire.

JOHNNYCAKES

While advancing across the ground near Burnside's Bridge, a Union soldier came across a dead Confederate whose haversack was full of "Johnny Cakes." The soldier emptied the cakes into his own pack and began to eat one. A friend turned to him and said it wasn't right to eat out of a dead man's haversack. The hungry soldier, his mouth full of cake, replied, "Damn 'em man, the Johnny is dead, but the Johnnycakes is not dead," and went right on eating.

NOT QUITE AS BAD

A Union sergeant named Henry Hubbard was struck by a bullet and knocked to the ground. His Captain bent down and asked the "apparently dying" man if he was badly hurt. "I guess I'm a goner this time, Cap," the sergeant replied with great difficulty. But when they went to find the wound they discovered that the bullet had simply dented his belt buckle and lodged in his cartridge box. "Hubbard was thoroughly disgusted at this commonplace ending to his adventure," saying it was "a mighty mean piece of business to pound a man most to death and not draw a drop of blood to show for it!"

THE LINE OF BATTLE

Dr. Hunter McGuire, of Stonewall Jackson's staff, was riding over the battlefield after the fighting. Near the Dunker Church he came upon a most curious spectacle.

I saw off at a distance in a field men lying down, and supposed it to be a line of battle.

I asked Colonel Grigsby why he did not move that line of battle back to make it conform to his own, when he said, "Those men...are all dead...They are Georgia soldiers."

Curiously, George H. Gordon, a Union soldier, recalls coming across a similar line, which quite possibly may have been the one described by Dr. McGuire:

In the dim light our guards came upon it.... "A line of battle here on duty!" exclaimed the officer in command; "there must be some mistake, for I was told that this would be my front, and here is a whole brigade of men..."

For some moments both officers and men were staggered at this mystery...

The sergeant now vainly attempted to arouse the man nearest him, with his foot; he stooped, shook the man, and cried out, "Halloo! I say! wake up!" Then the truth beginning to dawn upon him, he put his hand upon the head, the face, and found it cold; he listened, but heard no sound of life. Another: no answer! nor from another still, nor yet from any of those silent men lying there, stiff and stark, in the pale moonlight on that battlefield. Along the plain, over the hill, the line extended; until, lost in obscurity, nothing but dark masses appeared. Throughout the night the moon filled the scene with mystic images and unreal shapes. If phantoms from the spirit world could come forth to bewilder mortals, sure never was there time or place or sight so seasonable.... A whole brigade of Rebel dead lay there, a ghastly line of battle, as if they too were keeping watch upon the field.

THE "CHEW"

On the east side of the Antietam Creek, near Burnside's Bridge, three New York soldiers were casually talking while "occasionally dodging a shell" fired from Rebel cannon on the opposite bank. One of the men, "Butch" Sapher, wanted a "chew" but was out of tobacco. Just then the men spotted General Burnside himself passing by on his horse. The other men dared "Butch" to ask the General for a "chew." Without hesitation, Butch "jumped up, boldly strode towards him—saluted—and asked for the article desired. The general promptly reined in his horse and handed out his paper of fine cut, from which "Butch" abstracted an enormous chew, returning the paper with a "thank you, Gen'ral." The good-natured officer smiled and said, "Never mind. Keep it. You need it and I can get more."

East side of Burnside's Bridge, where "Butch" got his chew.

Barefoot Simonds

"Wesley Simonds, of Company I (9th New Hampshire), had the sole of one shoe cut completely off by a bullet, and then went around barefooted. By and by he volunteered to go on the skirmish line, and was starting off with 'one shoe off, and one shoe on,' when a comrade, noticing his sorry plight, said, 'Simonds, what are you going 'round barefoot for, when there's plenty of shoes lying 'round here, doing nobody any good?'

'Sure enough,' said Simonds; 'strange I never thought of that!' and a 'mate' if not a 'perfect fit' was soon found."

Hostile Patient

In the late afternoon of the seventeenth a wounded Confederate was carried into the yard of a "neat brick cottage" which was being used as a field hospital. Here he was placed next to another fallen comrade who graciously offered him his last sip of whiskey, which "wonderfully revived" the Reb. After drinking the whiskey, he asked his fellow soldier where he'd been hit. The soldier replied that "he had been shot through the knee by a piece of shell and that the surgeons wanted to amputate his leg, but, calling my attention to a pistol at his side, said, 'You see that? It will not be taken off while I can pull a trigger.' He entirely recovered, and led his battery into the next battle...

Compassionate Burnside

After a grueling day of fighting southeast of town, the men of Burnside's Ninth Corps had been driven back and held their ground at the edge of Antietam Creek. They held this position all through the night of the seventeenth and early morning of the eighteenth. As dawn broke, Burnside ordered cooked-rations sent to the front for his valiant troops. As soon as the men were relieved, however, they dropped from utter exhaustion and fell fast asleep. Shortly after Burnside rode to the front and "saw his meat on the Boards in a pile & he saw the troops asleep, [and with] the tears in his eyes...said, "It is rest they want first."

When the sun rose on the eighteenth of September, the scene that came to light was one of unspeakable horror. Mangled bodies of men and horses covered the field in every direction. The two battered armies held their ground and did their best to care for their wounded throughout the day. That night, under cover of darkness, the Confederate Army of Northern Virginia quietly slipped back across the Potomac River. Thousands of men, who had first waded the cool waters of that same river just 13 days earlier, were not among them.

PART IV

AFTERMATH
FLUKE TRUCE

All throughout the evening of the seventeenth and into the next day the two armies faced each other, covering themselves as best they could by hiding behind trees, rocks, dips in the ground or whatever else was available. Sometimes, in such places as the Cornfield, the lines were as close as one hundred yards from each other and incessant sniping took place at whoever showed any part of his body. It was here that men of the 29th Massachusetts found themselves at this time, listening to the awful moans and pleas of the wounded stranded between the lines. At times, men overcome by the cries for help would endanger their own lives by crawling out to comfort these unfortunates.

It was one of these missions of mercy which created a very interesting situation. A small group of these Massachusetts soldiers crawled out to rescue a wounded man, and as they slid the stretcher under him the enemy spotted part of the white canvas and took it to be a flag of truce. Immediately they ceased firing and in a short while a Confederate general appeared, to answer the supposed Union white flag. General Meager, on the Union side, now went out to meet the Rebel officer to see why he had called the truce. Soon, the two Generals began arguing about who had actually called the truce and after a "heated conversation" they returned to their own lines and the shooting began again. In the lull, however, the men of the 29th managed to get the wounded soldier back safely behind their lines.

THE BRUISE

The night of the battle, after the firing had stopped and the wounded were being cared for, a group of Federal soldiers who had their first taste of war that day were sitting around a camp fire. Naturally their talk turned to the events of the day, what they had seen and who amongst their friends had been hit or killed.

Then one of them, a soldier named Curtis Bowne, said, "By the way, I got a little dose of it myself. Look at this." Bowne then took of his hat and pointed to a small round bruise in the center of his forehead. The other boys leaned in to examine it in the flickering fire light.

"What is it?" asked one of the boys.

"I don't know. I think I must have been hit by a spent ball that just bruised the skin without entering."

"You are sure that it did not go into your brains?" remarked one of them laughingly.

"No!" answered Curtis good-naturedly. "My brains are not as soft as that."

"Does it hurt?"

"Not a bit. It is nothing—not worth talking about."

One of the soldiers who was sitting around that campfire that night, finishes the story:

> And none of us thought at the time that it was worth talking about. Yet at that very moment there was a one-ounce bullet imbedded in Curt Bowne's brain that afterward caused his death. He remained with the regiment for some days and then his head began to pain him so badly that he had to be sent to the hospital. He grew worse, but very slowly, and he actually lived until the following March, when he died from the effects of the wound which was at first supposed by all to be so trivial.
>
> The theory of the doctors...was that the bullet had passed between the convolutions of the brain without lacerating their coverings, that there was consequently no immediate hemorrhage, and that death resulted at last from slow inflammation.

STRANGE BEDFELLOW

It was common practice during the Civil War for soldiers to sleep under the same blanket during cold weather in order to share body warmth. At times, as many as five or six men would sleep side by side, one tucking the top of his legs against the bottom of the one in front of him and so on. This was called "spooning." The only problem was that when one of the men wanted to change position he would call out, "Roll over!" and the rest of his bed-mates would have to turn over as well.

At about two o'clock in the morning on the eighteenth, a New York sergeant decided to bed down for the night after many exhausting hours of caring for the wounded.

> I rejoined my company, and, as I had brought no blanket upon the field, thought I would share that of one of my own men, and quietly backed under the side of the blanket of a

sleeping soldier and presently went to sleep. Awakening at day-light and finding it time to call my company, I spoke to my host, and, getting no response, put my hand on his shoulder to arouse him. As he remained motionless I turned back the blanket, and saw a dead Confederate. I had enjoyed three or four hours of refreshing sleep, made comfortable by the warm blanket that covered us, but the chill I got from looking on my quiet bedfellow was greater, I believe, than I would have taken had I slept that cold night with nothing over me but the stars.

PANIC IN THE DARK

In studying the Civil War, or any war for that matter, one comes across many tales of a gruesome nature. But the following story is one of the most extreme of this type.

In the darkness of night, a soldier from New Jersey who had first experienced battle that very day, was drawn to a large barn from which an eerie sound was emanating. Upon investigation, the young volunteer found himself amidst a scene of indescribable horror which soon over-whelmed him.

The surgeons were in their shirt sleeves. The aprons that some of them wore were as red with blood as if they had been butchers. Assistants held candles to light the operation. I saw the doctor give one cut into the fleshy part of the man's thigh—and [then I] fled!

But I ran straight into another amputating table—a board over two barrels. Here they were taking off an arm! Turning, I ran against another! In every direction that I might go, I would run against one of the horrid things.

Blinded with fright and terror, I tried to escape...Seeing an apparently open way, I deliriously rushed in that direction, but meeting some obstruction, I stumbled and fell.

What had I fallen into? In grasping to steady myself, I caught hold of something wet and slimy! It was quite dark, but I could see! I could see all too plainly. Would to heaven I could not see!

I had fallen headlong into a heap of horrors—a pile of human legs and arms that had just been amputated. I shall not attempt to say how many there were. Were I to say there were a dozen wagon-loads of arms and legs, hands and feet, in that ghastly pile, I might not be believed!

And yet I do not believe it would be an exaggeration.

As I lay there, scrambling for a foothold in that slimy, slip-pery, bloody, hideous mass of human flesh—there arose from one of the operating tables another wild shriek:

"Oh, doctor! Oh! Oh-h! O-h-h-h! O-o-o-o-o-h! Kill me!
Kill me and be done with it! Kill me and put me out of my
misery!"

My overwrought brain could stand no more! I fainted!

I dropped unconscious into the slimy, slippery, bloody mass
of amputated legs and arms!"

THE GUN RESCUE

As the sun faded in the western sky the evening of the eighteenth,
a Confederate gunner named William Poague received orders from
General Jackson to retrieve a cannon which had somehow been stranded
between enemy lines. So, after dark, Poague and a small detail of
infantrymen cautiously approached their own picket lines and asked
where the gun was. "Right out there," whispered the picket in reply as
he pointed to the front, "not more than 75 or 100 yards."

Upon hearing this, the infantrymen decided it was not worth getting captured or shot over a single gun and despite Poague's "persua-
sion" and "threats" they refused to go a step beyond the picket line. So
Poague had to undertake this "ticklish job" with a small squad of his
own men. Off they went into "no-man's land," taking extreme caution
not to catch the Union pickets' attention. But they could not find the
gun. They began to think they had been misdirected when somehow,
"after groping around for some time" they "stumbled on it."

Now, a new problem arose. With all of the unsure wandering and
searching they had done in the dark, they could not remember which
direction would lead them back to their own lines. After discussing
their dilemma for a short time, they all came to the conclusion that the
gun was probably pointing towards the enemy. So, after "fixing things
as well as could be done to prevent rattling," they headed off in the
opposite direction, dragging the heavy gun behind.

Finally, after an arduous crawl through the awful aftermath of
battle, they reached their own lines "some distance" from where they
had started. The infantry men "now made no objection to hauling the
piece behind" the main line, and Poague's brave men were "done with
the disagreeable and hazardous affair."

THE AMPUTATION

In one of the many field hospitals after the battle, a member of the
9th Massachusetts was witness to this sad incident. Who knows how
many times this scene was repeated during those awful days?

A boy about fourteen years old was undergoing the process of amputation. He lay upon the stage, dressed in his Rebel
uniform, his face pale, and his large blue eyes gazing

wonderingly around. His injured leg was stretched before the surgeons, who were carefully feeling it about the wound—a black break, about the size of a nickel cent. A sign from one of the doctors, and the instruments were brought and placed upon a large box that once contained army clothes, but now was partly filled with bandages besmeared with blood. The surgeon selected one of the instruments; a cloth was held before the nostrils of the white-faced boy; the surgeon began his work. The skin of the white leg was cut; in a little while the bone was off, the arteries taken up, the skin laid over, the bandages applied, and the whole bound up carefully. "It is finished," said the doctor, as he wiped the blood from his hands. He said truly; the work was finished. *The boy was dead!*

The scene inside a barn near Antietam Creek, used as a field hospital. Note the amputation table set up just a few feet from the horse stables.

YANKEE SMARTNESS

In a Union field hospital after the battle, a captured Confederate surgeon was amputating the leg of one of his own men. On the doctor's collar was a shiny star indicating a rank of some sort. While he was operating he was also talking to a "tall, muscular man of the "Maine lumber species'" who was standing beside him. At one point the surgeon laid down a small pair of scissors which he had been using. The tall Yankee picked up the scissors and began to examine them. Then, turning his attention to the doctor, he quickly snipped the star from the Rebel's collar, and coolly walked away, whistling a patriotic tune.

The doctor did not notice his missing star for some time. When he finally did, he looked around for his "Yankee friend" but the Maine man was nowhere to be seen. Realizing he'd been had, he said, "Well, gentlemen, I've never been *north*, but I've heard a great deal about Yankee *smartness*, and wooden hams and nutmegs, and I concluded the 'Yanks' were pretty smart; but I never *did* think one of them smart enough to steal a star from under a man's chin before!"

LAST PRAYER

Shortly after the fighting ceased, army correspondent Charles Coffin was riding the field when he came upon this pitiful sight.

I recall a Union soldier lying near the Dunker Church with his face turned upward, and his pocket Bible open upon his breast. I lifted the volume and read the words: "Though I walk through the valley of the shadow of death, I will fear no evil; for Thou art with me. Thy rod and Thy staff, they comfort." Upon the fly leaf were the words; "We hope and pray that you may be permitted by a kind Providence, after the war is over, to return."

BAD TIMING

Ignatious Dufree, a resident of the Middletown Valley, apparently got caught up in the frenzy of war as the Rebel army marched through his town on September 13. Deciding to join their cause, off he marched with them that very day as a new recruit.

On the very next day occurred the savage fighting for South Mountain and three days later, bloody Antietam. That evening Ignatious returned home, perhaps now disillusioned by the image of war. The next day, however, for some unexplained reason, he went back to the battlefield and this time when he returned home he was "arrested as a spy and taken to Frederick for safekeeping."

CHILLING IMAGES

A Union soldier from Pennsylvania arrived on the scene with his regiment two days after the battle, and proceeded to march over Burnside's Bridge and through the town itself. His reminiscences many years later paint a hauntingly graphic portrait of the realities of war.

[We] passed over the hill where a Confederate battery was stationed. At this place we found their dead unburied. There were not less than 20 dead horses to be seen. One dead batteryman had his pockets full of apples and was eating them when killed by a cannon ball going thru his body, tearing away his left leg. His comrades had placed the torn-off member under his head as a pillow. This circumstance was often referred to by comrades.... Within a quarter of a mile of Sharpsburg our line halted. We suffered much from thirst, and I took a number of canteens of my comrades, and went into town. A gate standing open showed me a draw well. At the windlass was a dead man, his blood covering everything. I left the well in a hurry. A door was open; in the house lay two more dead men, a cannon ball having passed thru the corner of the house killing them. [This was the Smith House, located on the southwest corner of the alley on Main Street, opposite the old Lutheran graveyard.]

The next day the soldier came across a boy from Georgia who was only about 14 or 15 years old. The boy was crying.

He showed me his wound. It was a small wound on his wrist. I told him it was not dangerous. He said he was crying for his mother. I told him he would be allowed to go home. In two days I called to see him again and found he had died—hopelessly homesick.

HOPELESS CASE

By midnight of Wednesday most of the wounded who still had a chance for survival had been removed to field hospitals. Many of the "hopeless" cases, however, still remained on the field. These included men with severe head wounds or men shot through vital organs for whom nothing could be done. For them it was just a matter of time. As a reporter for the New York *Times* made his way across the battlefield he witnessed the last agonizing moments of one of these poor unfortunates. A Rebel soldier lay on the ground, trying vainly to rise. He clutched at the air as if to grab something to aid him. As the reporter drew closer to the man, however, he saw what had happened. On the side of the man's head, near the temple, was a large hole from which the soldier's "brain protruded." Someone reached out a helping hand and said words of sympathy but the soldier did not respond. And a moment later "the helpless victim fell over upon his face, and was numbered with the dead."

TERRIBLE WOUND

Any romantic notions of war are easily dispelled by the following story. It is but one of the thousands of horrific incidents that occurred in the field hospitals after the battle. This particular story happened to a member of the 108th New York at Antietam.

> ...Lieutenant Wm. W. Bloss came up to us, and getting between our knees, threw his head back and said: "For God's sake, jam a straw up my nose, I am strangling!" We were tender in jamming, and as the coagulated blood was choking him, he suddenly snatched the straw from our hand, and thrusting it up his nostrils, was speedily relieved of his distress.

Bloss had the bridge of his nose crushed by a bullet earlier in the day while holding the regiment's colors near the Sunken Road. For the rest of his life he was disfigured.

Smooth Operators

The night of the seventeenth, three Federal soldiers were assigned to guard twelve cattle which were to be slaughtered in the morning for beef. To make it easier, they decided that one would stay on watch for two hours while the other two slept, then another one would take watch, and so on. At one point in the night, the soldier who was supposed to be on watch nodded off, and when they awoke...the cattle were gone!

What to do? These men were all new recruits and had no idea what their punishment would be, but of course they all feared the worst. So, the men held a "council of war" and came to a conclusion— they had to find twelve more cattle to replace their missing ones.

So off they went into the dark fields and woods around Sharpsburg on their desperate mission. They passed "thousands of sleeping soldiers along the Hagerstown Pike" and saw plenty of cattle—all under the supervision of watchful guards. "If we don't strike a fat barnyard, we're lost," said one of the soldiers, starting to feel the pressure.

But find one they did, and in the darkness they quickly and as quietly as possible rounded up twelve cattle, along with a couple of "fine chickens," and returned to their post just before daylight. After herding the cattle into a corner, they relighted their campfire, and when the sun came up they looked as "innocent" as if they had faithfully done their duty all night.

At nine o'clock, the relief arrived to take charge of the cattle. "How's this?" asked the officer of the new guard.

"How's what?" replied one of the cattle thieves, a Wisconsin corporal.

"This order says that you are to be relieved of the charge of twelve steers. And these are cows. And let me see," the officer began counting, "why, there are thirteen of them! How's that?"

In that dark barnyard the night before the soldiers had made a couple of slight mistakes which only now did they come to realize. The Wisconsin corporal was not ruffled, however, and coolly said, "Don't know nothing about it, lieutenant. Them there's the critters we had turned over to us. I didn't count 'em. Guess the other fellows must have made a mistake."

"But they're cows, not steers. And you ought to know that the government never kills cows for beef."

"Don't know nothing about that, neither. If them was steers yesterday they must have changed during the night somehow, for they're cows now sure enough. It am a curious circumstance, I vow."

The officer didn't see the point in arguing any further and let the men go on their way.

As soon as the men got far enough away, the corporal exclaimed, "Dash my buttons. I wish some of you fellows would give me a good kick."

"What for?" asked one of the soldiers.

"Don't you see? We had one critter too many, and we might ha' killed her and had fried brains for our breakfast. And then did you see them udders? We might ha' had milk in our coffee. Kick me for a fool!"

ANSWERING A BROTHER'S PLEA

Early on the morning of the eighteenth, the Fifth New Hampshire was doing picket duty in the cornfield just south of the Bloody Lane. Suddenly, one of the pickets heard a soft voice come out of the corn, crying for help. When he investigated, he found a wounded Confederate soldier who was covered in blood. The Rebel then handed him a little slip of paper. On it the man had used a piece of cornstalk, dipped in his own blood, and with great difficulty drawn some mystic signs in a circle. The wounded man begged the Union soldier to find some Freemason [a member of a fraternal brotherhood] as soon as possible and show him the paper.

The New Hampshire man then brought the strange message to Colonel Cross of his regiment who was a Master Mason. The colonel could not read the message, however, and sent for Captain J. B. Perry who was a Freemason of a higher degree. Upon reading it, Captain Perry immediately reacted, saying there was a "brother Mason in great peril, and must be rescued." Colonel Cross then sent word to several other Masons in the regiment and soon "four 'brothers of the mystic tie' were crawling stealthily through the corn to find their brother in distress. He was found, placed on a blanket, and at great risk drawn out of the range of Rebel sharpshooters, and then carried to the Fifth New Hampshire hospital."

The man turned out to be First Lieutenant Edon of the Alabama Volunteers. He was badly wounded in the thigh and chest and would have surely died in a few hours. The Lieutenant then told of another brother Mason, a Lieutenant Colonel of a Georgia regiment, who was also lying wounded in the corn. That man was then found and brought in. "These two officers received the same attention as the wounded officers of the Fifth, and a warm friendship was established between men who, a few hours before, were in mortal combat."

THE OPEN WINDOW

"After the battle of Antietam a recruit, one of those who had joined the regiment about a week previous, wandered off to see what he could discover that was new. In his rambles he came to a large house, and seeing an open window, he approached it to gratify his curiosity as to what was inside of it, when, as his head raised above the sill, the gory stump of a man's arm was thrust in his face, with the remark, "Young man, take this away and bury it." That recruit returned to the regiment a sick man. He had run across one of the hospitals where the wounded were being attended to."

The Smith House northeast of Sharpsburg being used as a hospital.

Courtesy of William A. Frassanito, *Antietam: The Photographic Legacy of America's Bloodiest Day.*

THE GEORGIAN'S EXCUSE

Shortly after the battle, a Georgia soldier was confronted by his commanding officer and asked to explain his absence during the fighting. He replied by saying that he just couldn't keep up with the army on the grueling, fast-paced march to Sharpsburg. "I had no shoes," he said. "I tried it barefoot, but somehow my feet wouldn't callous. They just kept bleeding. I found it so hard to keep up that though I had the heart of a patriot, I began to feel I didn't have patriotic feet. Of course,

I could have crawled on my hands and knees, but then my hands would have got so sore I couldn't have fired my rifle."

A Bowl of Gruel

Situated directly across the Potomac River from Sharpsburg, sits the quiet little town of Sheperdstown, West Virginia (at the time of the battle it was still Virginia). Because of its proximity to the fighting as well as being the avenue of Lee's escape, this small town saw massive transformation in those awful September days. By Thursday, every barn, building and home had become a hospital. The wounded occupied every inch of space, and were overflowing into the streets. The townspeople labored day and night in caring for the wounded and as they worked wagonloads of wounded men were carried in from the fields.

On Friday, September 19, Lee's army occupied the town. Across the river, the Union artillery lobbed shells toward the town, trying to do further damage to the Confederates. A woman of Sheperdstown relates his incident, which occurred in an old building along the river:

> A friend who worked chiefly in the old blue factory had asked me to bring her a bowl of gruel that someone had promised to make for one of her patients. I had just taken it to her, and she was walking across the floor with the bowl in her hands, when a shell crashed through a corner of the wall and passed out at the opposite end of the building, shaking the rookery to its foundations, filling the room with dust and plaster, and throwing her upon her knees to the floor. The wounded screamed, and had they not been entirely unable to move, not a man would have been left in the building. But it was found that no one was hurt, and things proceeded as before. I asked her afterward if she was frightened. She said yes, when it was over, but her chief thought at the time was to save the gruel, for the man needed it, and it had been very hard to find any one composed enough to make it. I am glad to be able to say that he got his gruel in spite of bombs.

No Hurry

On the nineteenth of September, two days after the battle, the 20th Maine was ordered to cross the Potomac River into Sheperdstown to follow after Lee's retreating army. After battling the swift currents of the river the Maine boys scrambled up the banks toward the sound of increasing gun-fire. At the top, they quickly drew the attention of the

Rebels and a brisk exchange of firing ensued. The regiment was about to charge, when suddenly they were ordered back across the river.

So, back down the steep bank they hastily scrambled and eventually back to the Maryland shore. There was a man in the ranks of the 20th Maine by the name of Tommy Welch. Welch was a "brave, generous hearted fellow," 42 years of age. He was "one of those funny, neat, particular men," who was "always making the most laughable blunders, and was usually behind all others in obeying any command." The boys used to joke that he would "rather sacrifice the whole army of the Potomac, than to have a spot of rust upon his rifle, or dust upon his uniform."

During this mad scramble, the rest of the men had all reached the river before Tommy knew what was happening, and then he "very slowly descended, picking his path carefully among the trees and rocks, and did not reach the river until the rear of the regiment was nearly halfway across." The commander of the regiment sat on his horse in the river and patiently waited for Tommy. But when Tommy reached the river bank, amongst the "zip-zip" of bullets in the air, he sat down a rock, removed his shoes and socks, and "slowly packed them away in his blanket." By now the bullets were getting thicker, nipping the water and banging off rocks. But Tommy now proceeded to roll his pant legs up over his knees so he wouldn't get them wet. He stood up, took a few steps, and his pants slipped back down. So Tommy retraced his steps to the shore to roll them up again. The commanding officer, still on his horse in the river called out, "Come, come, my man, hurry up, hurry up, or we will both be shot!"

Tommy looked up with a "Serio-comic gravity of expression" and called back in his Irish accent, "The divil a bit, sur. It is no mark of a gintlemen to be in a hurry."

The officer now spurred his horse to safety, and Tommy Welch "carrying his rifle in one hand, and holding up his pant legs in the other, followed after, the bullets flying thickly all around him," and made it safely across the river.

SWEET SAD SONG

In a barn being used as a temporary hospital, the following scene occurred:

Among the wounded men here, was a poor soldier, both of whose legs had been amputated. He had been told by the surgeons that his case was a hopeless one, and if he had any message to send to his friends in the North, they would gladly transmit the same. He then dictated to the surgeons a brief, but touching, letter to his wife and family.... After talking a few moments, he asked those about him to raise his head from the floor. Suddenly summoning all his remaining energies, he began to sing in a clear and very melodious voice, "Home Sweet Home." All voices save his were quickly hushed...The surgeons and nurses who were on duty among the wounded paused in their labors, and stood spell-bound and fascinated by the sweetness of his voice...The appearance of the dying singer, his countenance pallid and bloodless, gave the spectacle a strange, unearthly character, and the effective rendering which he gave to the tender and touching sentiment of the song fairly melted the hearts of all present; and when he finished, breathing out in utterance of the closing words the last remnant of his strength, and sank almost senseless upon his pallet, "there was not a dry eye in the room." The poor soldier died in the course of the day....

PILED BODIES

Many visitors to the battlefield just after the battle remembered seeing men piled in heaps, sometimes as many as five deep. They attributed this to the men falling so thickly where they were shot down. This description may be a bit misleading. A member of the 53rd Pennsylvania remembered that while on picket duty near the Bloody Lane (where the observation tower now stands) they were dangerously exposed to the deadly fire of the Rebel sharpshooters. For protection, they gathered bodies of the dead and piled them in front of them. According to the Pennsylvania soldier, this is what those early visitors actually saw, although in some stretches of Bloody Lane there were heaps of bodies two to three deep.

RECOLLECTIONS

Many years after the battle, a hired man who was living at the Jacob Nicodemus Farm, north of the Dunker Church, remembered the horrible aftermath of the fighting:

> All over the fields the bodies was picked up, but those right around the buildings was left. I suppose the soldiers thought that the people who owned the buildings would bury the bodies to get rid of 'em. It was a warm September. Yes, sir, some days was very hot, and we had to bury them bodies or stand the stench. By Saturday night I had all those on our place buried, but the smell hung on for a month, there was so many dead men and horses that was only half covered. The stench was sickening. We couldn't eat a good meal, and we

had to shut the house up just as tight as we could of a night to keep out that odor. We couldn't stand it, and the first thing in the morning when I rolled out of bed I'd have to take a drink of whiskey. If I didn't I'd throw up before I got my clothes all on....

Another queer thing was the silence after the battle. You couldn't hear a dog bark nowhere, you couldn't hear no birds whistle or no crows caw. There wa'n't no birds around till the next spring. We didn't even see a buzzard with all that stench. The rabbits had run off, but there was a few around that winter—not many. The farmers didn't have no chickens to crow. Our'n didn't commence for six months. When night come I was so lonesome that I didn't know what lonesome was before. It was a curious silent world.

Confederate dead along the Hagerstown Pike.

Courtesy of William A. Frassanito, *Antietam: The Photographic Legacy of America's Bloodiest Day.*

HENRY'S "BRILLIANT" IDEA

Henry Burrier, a citizen of nearby Middletown, Maryland, visited the battlefield in early October. As he walked the fields he came across three unexploded shells which he scooped up and brought home as souvenirs of the great battle. Upon closer examination, he discovered that his "trophies" were covered with unsightly rims of lead. Well, Henry could not have this, so to solve the problem he simply put the shells into his kitchen stove and went about his business, thinking that when he returned the lead would be melted off.

71

Meanwhile, the unsuspecting Mrs. Burrier was busy washing clothes outside, just a few feet away from the stove full of shells. Suddenly, without warning,

> bang!—one of these missiles of death bursted, tearing the stove, part of the chimney place and furniture of the room to pieces, and a portion of it falling into the wash tub. 'Vexed but not disconcerted, Mrs. Burrier scolded a little at her husband for putting these foolish things in the fire,' and taking up the tongs pulled the other two shells, which were pretty well heated, out of the coals, and threw them into the street.

Miraculously, she was unhurt, due to the massive chimney between her and the stove at the time of the explosion.

"SUCH A SOIL"

The following is an article from a local newspaper. The "matter-of fact" style is an eerie testimonial to the more pragmatic effect the battle had on those local farmers, whose land would be forever changed.

> The fields over which the battles of Antietam raged are dotted in every direction with graves. These graves are generally very shallow, and it will be difficult hereafter to turn up the soil to any depth without disturbing the bones of those who repose in them. Many unexploded shells have also buried themselves beneath the surface, and if these should come in violent contact with the plow cutter they would certainly explode, and render ploughing a very unsafe work in such a soil.

IMPROPER BURIALS

Although we will never know the exact figure, it has been estimated that 3,654 men were killed outright in one day at the Battle of Antietam. This staggering number does not include the thousands that would die in the following days, weeks, and even months after the battle. Needless to say, the task of burying these thousands of bloated, decomposing bodies was overwhelming. Because of this, the burial techniques were often crude and ineffective. In many places, and especially after a rainfall, legs, heads, and arms could be seen poking up out of the earth.

In mid-October of 1862, Mr. C.M. Keedy, a "well-known man" of nearby Keedysville visited the battlefield. He remembered in one place a group of dead soldiers that had simply been laid on the ground with rails placed around them and some loose dirt piled on. The hogs had "rooted the shoes off with feet still in them." He also remembered that for several years it was not uncommon to see human bones lying around in gutters and fence corners, or hogs walking about with limbs clenched in their teeth.

A young Confederate lies dead next to a freshly dug Union grave.

Courtesy of William A. Frassanito, *Antietam: The Photographic Legacy of America's Bloodiest Day.*

THE ARM

About two and a half weeks after the battle, a local farmer was plowing in his field when he noticed a strange object lying in one of his freshly plowed rows. Upon closer examination he discovered that it was a human hand and forearm. Deciding to keep it as a souvenir of the recent battle, he put the arm in a barrel of salt-brine to preserve it. Six months later, the farmer decided that he didn't want the arm, and gave it to a physician in town.

The physician transferred the arm into a formaldehyde solution which more thoroughly completed the preservation process. Seventy years went by and in 1937, after the doctor had passed away, his possessions were to be sold. Among his effects, found in the attic of his Boonsboro home, was a wrapped piece of cloth. Inside the cloth was the arm, its skin and fingernails still perfectly preserved.

Twenty years later, in 1957, the arm came into the possession of a Sharpsburg resident who owned a small antique shop/museum. He mounted the arm in a glass display case on the wall of his museum room. That arm can still be seen today, in the same case, in the same antique shop in Sharpsburg, Maryland, now under new ownership. The arm is judged to be that of a nineteen year old boy.

HEAVY CORPSE

In 1866, the tremendous task of disinterring bodies for their move to the new national cemetery began. Among those participating in this gruesome work was Sharpsburg resident Elias Spong, himself a veteran of the war. Elias had just unearthed a body near the East Woods on the David Miller Farm when, while trying to lift him, he realized the man seemed extremely heavy for his size. Turning him over, he found a twelve pound cannonball imbedded in the man's bowels.

THE RING

Some time after the battle, Governor Curtin of Pennsylvania was traveling through Philadelphia when he was introduced to a young woman. The woman, extremely happy to see the Governor, reached up and planted a kiss on his forehead. The governor was completely taken by surprise. "Madam," he said with a smile, "to whom am I indebted for this unexpected salutation?"

"Sir, do you not know me?" she replied.

The governor said he didn't and offered her a chair. As they sat, the young woman continued, "Shortly after the battle of Antietam, you were upon that bloody field."

"I was," said the Governor.

"You administered to the wants of the wounded and the dying."

"It was my duty as a feeling man."

"You did your duty well. Heaven alone will reward you, sir, for in this life there is no reward adequately expressive of your deserts. You, sir, imparted consolation and revived the hopes of a dying soldier of the Twenty-eighth Ohio. He was badly wounded in the arm; you lifted him into an ambulance, and the blood dripping from him stained your hands and your clothing. That soldier was as dear to me as life itself."

"What it your husband?" asked the Governor.

"No, sir," the woman replied.

"A brother perhaps?"

"No, sir."

The Governor continued his questioning: a father? a son? a lover? To each of these, the woman answered no. The Governor was perplexed. "If not a husband, father, brother, son, or lover, who, then, could it be? This is an enigma to me. Please explain more about the gallant soldier of Ohio."

"Well, sir, that soldier gave you a ring. C.E.D. were the letters engraved on the interior. That is the ring now upon your little finger. He told you to wear it, and carefully have you done so."

The Governor removed the ring and looked at the inside of the band. Sure enough, there were the letters.

The woman went on, "The finger that used to wear that ring will never wear it any more. The hand is dead, but the soldier still lives."

The Governor's curiosity was now at a peak. "Well, madam, tell me about it. Is this ring yours? Was it given to you by a soldier whom you loved?"

"I loved him as I loved my life; but he never returned that love. He had more love for his country than for me; I honor him for it. That soldier who placed that ring upon your finger stands before you." The strange woman then rose and showed the Governor her arm, which had been amputated part way down, and had been previously concealed.

The two spent the next hour chatting amiably. Her name was Catherine E. Davidson and she was from Sheffield, Ohio. Before the war, she had been engaged to be married but when President Lincoln called for volunteers, her fiancee enlisted. Not being able to stand the separation from her beloved, she enlisted in another regiment, disguised as a man.

On the seventeenth of September, 1862, however, her dreams were tragically and permanently shattered. Her fiancee was killed and she herself was wounded in the fighting near Burnside's Bridge as a member of the 28th Ohio Volunteer Infantry. It was a strange war.

THE SOURCES

PART I

A Rude Awakening; Jones, Paul. *The Irish Brigade*. Washington: Robert B. Luce Inc., 1969.

Grabbing the Bull by the Horns; Lord, E. O. *History of the 9th Regiment of New Hampshire Volunteers*. Concord: Republican Press, 1895.

Cow and Calf; Cockrell, M. F. *Gunner with Stonewall*. Wilmington, NC: Broadfoot Publishing, 1987.

Sleepy Stonewall; *Frederick Examiner*, September 24, 1862.

A Scrap Over Water; Hitchcock, Col. Frederick L. *War From the Inside*. Philadelphia: 1904.

A Macabre Gift; Harwell, R. B. *The Union Reader*. New York: Longmans, Green, and Co., 1958.

A Maryland Maiden Reconsiders; Ward, J. E. D. *The 12th Ohio Infantry*. Ripley, Ohio: 1864.

Rails; Hutchinson, Nelson V. *History of the 7th Massachusetts Volunteers*. Taunton, MA: 1890.

A Bit Too Cocky; *Middletown Valley Register*, September 19, 1862.

Dirty Army; *New York Times*, September 14, 1862.

Strange Boast; *New York Times*, September 14, 1862.

Mad Lantz; Harrer, William. *With Drum and Gun in '61*. Greenville, PA: Beaver Printing, 1908.

"Damnably Deceived"; *New York Times*, September 16, 1862.

Fine Business; *New York Times*, September 14, 1862.

Jackson and Brandy; Tate, Allen. *Stonewall Jackson, The Good Soldier*. New York: Minton, Bach, and Co., 1928.

Late Night Feast; Bradford, Ned. *Battles and Leaders of the Civil War*. New York: The Century Co., 1888.

Horse For Sale; Harwell. *The Union Reader*. New York: Longman's, Green, & Co., 1958.

Dinner at a "Reb" House; Hitchcock. *War From the Inside*.

The General's Kiss; Hitchcock. *War From the Inside*.

Confederate Punishment; Stone, J. M. *Personal Recollections of the Civil War*. Boston: 1918.

Where's John Conley?; Lane, David. *A Soldier's Diary*. Michigan: 1905.

PART II

Strange Coincidence; *Middletown Valley Register*. October 3, 1862.

The Tree; Brinkerhoff, Lt. Henry R. *History of the 13th Ohio*. Columbus, OH: Osgood, 1863.

Deadly Dilemma; Ward, J. E. D. *12th Ohio Infantry.* Ripley, OH: 1864.

Jarred Jokester; Priest, J. M. *Captain James Wren's Civil War Diary.* New York: Berkley Books, 1990.

One on One; Fairchild, C. B. *27th Regiment N.Y. Vols.* Bingamton, NY: Carl and Matthews, 1888.

Brave Rebel Color Sergeant; Ward. *12th Ohio Infantry.*

A Young Yankee Loses His Nerve; Bicknell, G. W. *History of the 5th Maine Volunteers.* Portland, ME: Hall L. Davis, 1871.

Eerie Premonition; Cheek, Philip. *History of the Sauk County Riflemen.* Wisconsin: 1909.

Knapsacks; Priest. *Wren's Diary.*

Confused "Billy" Fitzpatrick; Priest. *Wren's Diary.*

A Confederate Surrenders; Smith, A. P. *History of the 76th N. Y. V.* Cortland, NY: 1867.

Brave Decision; Smith. *History of the 76th N. Y. V.*

Rebel Boots; Lord. *History of the 9th New Hampshire.*

Hospital Scene; Priest. *Wren's Diary.*

The Old Cock; Carter, Robert G. *Four Brothers in Blue.* Austin, TX: University of Texas Press, 1913.

Goodbye; Moe, Richard. *The Last Full Measure.* New York: Henry Holt and Co., 1993.

Sergeant French's Conversation; Jackman, Lyman. *History of the 6th New Hampshire.* Concord: Republican Press, 1891.

Last Words; Galwey, Thomas F. *The Valiant Hours.* Harrisburg, PA: The Stackpole Company, 1961.

The Best Hit; Walcott, C. F. *History of the 21st Massachusetts Volunteers.* Boston: Houghton, Mifflin Co., 1882.

The Well; Walcott. *History of the 21st Massachusetts.*

Quick-Thinking Chaplain; Kramer, Samuel. *Maryland and the Glorious Third.* Washington: 1882.

The Big Speculation; Worsham, J. H. *One of Jackson's Foot Cavalry.* New York: Neale Publishing, 1912.

The Heartless Lieutenant; Thomson, Orville. *From Philipi to Appomattox.* Indiana: 1900

Shopping; Eisenschiml and Newman. *The American Iliad.* New York: Grosset and Dunlap, 1947.

PART III

A Drink of Wine; Reilly, Oliver T. *Battlefield of the Antietam.* Sharpsburg, MD: 1906.

Brotherly Love; Carleton and soldiers of New England. *Stories of Our Soldiers.* Boston: *Boston Journal,* 1893.

Hiding Place; Reilly. *Battlefield of the Antietam.*

Defending the Flag Johnson, Clifton. *Battleground Adventures*. New York: Houghton Mifflin, 1915.

Them Bursting Lamp-Posts; Donald, David. *Divided We Fought*. New York: MacMillan, 1956.

To Catch a Thief; Johnson. *Battleground Adventures*.

The Dog; Child, William. *History of the 5th Regiment New Hampshire Volunteers*. Bristol, NH: R. W. Musgrove, 1893.

Not A Baseball; Coffin, C. Carleton. *Battles and Leaders of the Civil War*. Vol. II. New York: The Century Co., 1888.

Strange Missiles at Antietam; Moore, Frank. *Anecdotes, Poetry, and Incidents*. New York: *The Rebellion Record*, 1866.

Rations; Murphey, Rev. T.G. *History of the First Delaware*. Philadelphia, PA: Claxton, 1866.

"A Gibe About Soap"; Blackford, W. W. *War Years With Stuart*. New York: Charles Scribner's Sons, 1945.

Breakfast is Interrupted; Johnson. *Battleground Adventures*.

Chaos in the Streets; Johnson. *Battleground Adventures*.

Upsetting Shot; Stone. *Personal Recollections*.

Mother Hubbards; Blackford. *War Years*.

No Respect; Moore, Frank. *The Story of a Cannoneer Under Stonewall Jackson*. New York: Neale Publishing, 1907.

Running for Cover; Moore. *Cannoneer*.

Lunch Meat; Mills, John H. *Chronicles of the 21st New York Volunteers*. Buffalo, NY: 1887.

Stonewall's Tree-Top Scout; Reilly. *Battlefield of the Antietam*.

Lieutenant White; *Stories of Our Soldiers*. Boston Journal, 1893.

Close Calls; *Stories of Our Soldiers*. Boston Journal, 1893.

The Disguise; Crowell, Joseph E. *The Young Volunteer*. New York: G. W. Dillingham, 1906.

Captain Bachelle's Dog; Dawes, R. R. *Combat: The Civil War*. New York: Dell, 1967.

The Unarmed Sergeant; Cooke, B. F. *History of the 12th Massachusetts*. Boston: 1882.

Battery Horses; Blackford. *War Years*., Moore. *Cannoneer*.

The Bayonet; Ellis, Thomas T. *Leaves from the Diary of an Army Surgeon*. New York: John Bradburn, 1863.

The Skedaddler; Brown, Edmund. *27th Indiana Volunteers*. Monticello, IN: 1899.

A Soldier Staggers; Moore, *Anecdotes*.

A Brave Man; *History of the 19th Massachusetts*. Salem, MA: Salem Press, 1906.

Religion Under Fire; Kohl, L. F. *Memoirs of a Chaplain's Life*. New York: Fordham University Press, 1992.

Brother Befriends Brother; *History of the 1st Minnesota.* Stillwater, Minnesota: 1916.

The Feeling of a Wound; Frederick, Gilbert. *57th New York State Vol. Inf.* New York: 57th Veteran Assoc., 1895.

Cheering the Boys Up; *The 19th Massachusetts.* Salem, MA: Salem Press, 1906.

Nervous Private Lloyd; Galwey. *The Valiant Hours.*

No Fear; Hitchcock. *War From the Inside.*

Deadly Mercy; Seville, W. P. *History of the First Delaware.* Wilmington, DE: Historical Society, 1882.

Nine and Ten; MacNamara, D. G. *History of the 9th Masssachusetts.* Boston: E. B. Stillings and Co., 1899.

Mother and Child; Reilly. *Battlefield of the Antietam.*

Father and Son; Wheeler, Richard. *Voices of the Civil War.* New York: Crowell Co., 1976.

Hot Seat; Donald, David. *Divided We Fought.* New York: MacMillan, 1956.

The Pick Pocket; Eisenschiml. *The American Iliad.*

I Knew I Was Gone; Wheeler. *Voices.*

Rebel Target; Hitchcock. *War From the Inside.*

Brave Yankee Rascal; Linderman, Gerald. *Embattled Courage.* New York: Free Press, 1987.

War Paint; Livermore, Thomas L. *Days and Events 1860-1866.* Boston: Houghton, Mifflin, 1920.

In a Pinch; Livermore. *Days and Events.*

Grisly Sight; Galwey. *The Valiant Hours.*

Bloody Lane; Coffin, C. C. *Battles and Leaders of the Civil War.* Vol. II. New York, NY: Century Co., 1884.

A Shot for Hill; Longstreet, General James. *From Manassas to Appomattox: Memoirs of the Civil War in America.* Philadelphia, PA: J. B. Lippincott, 1896.

The Can; Carter, R. G. *Four Brothers in Blue.* Austin, TX: University of Texas Press, 1913.

A Dreadful Spectacle; Thompson, David. *Blue and Gray.* New York, NY: Bobbs-Merril, 1950.

Poor Reb; Douglas, H. K. *I Rode With Stonewall.* Chapel Hill, NC: University of North Carolina Press, 1940.

Wise-Cracking "Tar-Heel"; Douglas, H. K. *I Rode With Stonewall.*

Brave Miss Miller; Douglas, H. K. *I Rode With Stonewall.*

Freaks of War; Lord. *History of the 9th New Hampshire.*

Hostile Patient; Moore. *Cannoneer.*

Scared Stiff; Lord. *History of the 9th New Hampshire.*

The Ride; Lord. *History of the 9th New Hampshire.*

Johnny-Cakes; Priest. *Wren's Diary.*

Not Quite as Bad; Cooke. *12th Massachusetts.*

The Line of Battle; Gordon, George H. *A War Diary.* Boston: J. R. Osgood, 1882. Bowers, J. *Stonewall Jackson: Portrait of a Soldier.* New York: W. Morrow & Co., 1989.

The Chew; Cowtan, Charles. *Services of the 10th N. Y. V.* New York: 1882.

Strange Bedfellow; Curtis, Newton. *Bull Run to Chancellorsville.* New York: G. P. Putnam and Sons, 1906.

Barefoot Simonds; Lord. *History of the 9th New Hampshire.*

Compassionate Burnside; Priest. *Wren's Diary.*

PART IV

Fluke Truce; Osborne, W. H. *History of the 29th Massachusetts.* Boston: Albert Wright, 1877.

The Bruise; Crowell. *The Young Volunteer.*

The Amputation; MacNamara, M. H. *The Irish Ninth in Bivouac and Battle.* Boston: Lee & Shepard, 1867.

The Gun Rescue; Cockrell. *Gunner With Stonewall.*

Yankee Smartness; MacNamara. *The Irish Ninth.*

Last Prayer; Coffin. *Battles and Leaders...* Vol II.

Bad Timing; *Middletown Valley Register.* September 19, 1862.

Chilling Images; Alexander, Ted. *The 126th Pennsylvania.* Shippensburg, PA: Beidel Printing House, 1984.

Hopeless Case; *New York Times.* September 21, 1862.

Terrible Wound; Washburn, George. *A Complete History of the 108th New York.* Rochester, NY: 1894.

Smooth Operators; Crowell. *The Young Volunteer.*

Answering a Brother's Plea; Moore. *Anecdotes.*

The Open Window; Davenport, Alfred. *Camp and Field: Life of the 5th New York.* New York: 1879.

A Georgian's Excuse; Botkin, B. A. *A Civil War Treasury.* New York: Random House, 1960.

No Hurry; Gerrish, Theodore. *Army Life: A Private's Reminiscences.* Portland, ME: Hoyt, Fogg, and Donham, 1882.

Sweet Sad Song; Osborne. *History of the 29th Massachusetts.*

Piled Bodies; Reilly. *Battlefield of the Antietam.*

Recollections Johnson. *Battleground Adventures.*

Henry's "Brilliant" Idea; *Middletown Valley Register.* October 17, 1862.

"Such a Soil"; *Middletown Valley Register.* October 3, 1862.

Improper Burials; Reilly. *Battlefield of the Antietam.*

The Arm; Mr. John Ray, Antietam Battlefield Civil War Museum, Sharpsburg, MD, personal interview, July 5, 1996.

Heavy Corpse; Reilly. *Battlefield of the Antietam.*

The Ring; Moore. *Anecdotes.*

The Lutheran Church in Sharpsburg shows the scars of Federal artillery fire.

Courtesy of William A. Frassanito, *Antietam: The Photographic Legacy of America's Bloodiest Day.*